THE COMMON SENSE APPROACH TO SELL REAL ESTATE

Carl Slade

Carl is the founder of Restate Ltd
Licensed Real Estate Agent (REAA 2008).
16 Church Street, Timaru 7910
New Zealand.

enq@restate.nz
www.Restate.nz

For specific comments or feedback regarding this book email:
carl@restate.nz

First published and printed in New Zealand 2016

ISBN: 978-0-473-38218-6

Cover design and typesetting: Caleb McAndrew at BookPrint Ltd.
'No Thanks' Cartoon by: Royce Art n Designs NZ Ltd

A NOTE TO READERS

Thank you. I'm honoured you have chosen to pick up this book and I certainly hope you find it eye-opening.

I'd like this to be a frank conversation. As if I was talking with a loved one – a good friend, my mother, or one of my children wanting to sell their home – where I can openly share some insights, with no agenda other than helping you as best I can.

A book however, can never be a real conversation. From this side of the page I can't possibly know your past experiences, understandings, or current situation. I can't see your reaction to a point made or a question posed. I can't hear your concerns or calls for further explanation. Instead I have to make assumptions about what you may be feeling, thinking or wanting to know. I will therefore do my best to stick to what I believe is most important for you to understand.

If there was one thing I could ask of you, it would be this: for you to engage. Turn this into a real conversation by sharing your thoughts, questions and reactions. If I've done a good job helping you – I want to know. If I've done a terrible job – I want to know. If you feel I have left out something important, or you have unanswered questions, then don't be shy.

Send your questions, thoughts and feedback to: carl@restate.nz

INTRODUCTION

This may not be the conventional way to start a book, especially one written by a real estate agent. Apparently I'm supposed to draw you in with some engaging 'origin story' or 'intriguing narrative' designed to hook you in. But if I were you - I would prefer you just talked straight. I also believe you are better served with some common sense truths that can empower you to beat the odds.

So I promise this book will not be your typical real estate industry propaganda. Instead, it pokes some rather obvious holes in the way the traditional industry works. It questions the status quo, challenges the establishment and calls for some common sense thinking.

As well as opening your eyes, I am hopeful this message will resonate with some agents, inspiring them to join the cause. But I am realistic. Most traditional agents are going to dismiss it as heresy. There may even be book burnings. It exposes truths that rattle the very foundations of what they have been led to believe is the *way*, and when we blindly follow a way, anything that questions that becomes a threat to our identity, which we fiercely fight to protect.

With that said, I did not write this for agents. It's for you, home sellers who have had enough of the way the industry works, who just want to sell your property without having to worry about whether or not you are being taken advantage of, who want an industry you can trust, one that protects your interests and genuinely helps you keep more of your hard-earned equity.

My motive is simple. I believe once you understand how this industry really works and can see the solution easily within your grasp, you will demand what you rightfully deserve. I hope these common sense truths, once revealed, will spark a revolution of sorts – an uprising – leading to a better industry for all.

Above all, I encourage you to take the reins of your sale back into your own hands. Without knowing it, you, the home seller, hold the ultimate power in real estate.

STOP. Read that again. Let it sink in for a moment. It will set you free... You, the home seller, hold the ultimate power in real estate.

I propose we reject the hype, gimmicks and lines pitched by the traditional industry. Let's apply some common sense and have a good look at how this industry really works. Let's state what we all know to be true but have failed to do anything about: there is an underlying force in real estate constantly working against us, robbing you of your trust and equity, and agents of their dignity.

Let's name that force, accept it as our enemy and look at how you can overcome it.

CONTENTS

PART ONE
Exposing How The Industry Really Works

Understanding the problem is the first
step to finding the solution.

CHAPTER ONE

FUNDAMENTAL TRUTHS

COMMON SENSE TRUTH #1
You hold the ultimate power in real estate

You hold the power: it all starts and ends with you. You, sellers, are the reason the industry exists. You are the paying client. Therefore you, and only you, can demand it serves you better. That is, only if you want it to. You are welcome to stick with the way it is. That is your choice.

Ask yourself: does the traditional model give you what you want? Can you trust its agents to act in your best interests? Are the fees you pay fair value for the services provided?

Unfortunately, for the large majority of home sellers, the answer to those questions is a resounding NO. It's no secret that real estate is among the least trusted industries in the world. And it's no surprise that the large majority of home sellers consider the commissions charged to be less than good value.

Those are facts, and regardless of what the industry says while trying to defend itself, there is no disputing how you (home sellers) feel.

The industry certainly talks the talk. Agents *say* they are working for you, will act in your best interests, get you the best price and so on. But you're not so sure who they are really working for. You can sense something lurking in the shadows. Lets turn on the light and have a good look.

A sales culture is self-serving

The real estate industry is built on a commission-only business model – driven by a sales culture. This foundation is the underlying force responsible for every problem you can think of with this industry. It's why you question the industry's integrity, and why the fees are so disconnected from the work actually done on your behalf. A sales culture is *self-serving*. It's about what's best for them instead of what's best for you. But you know this. You see it every day.

Survival trumps ethics

"Face the facts, you are now viewed as a 'Profession' and therefore required to act like one"…

were Michael's opening words as over 50 real estate salespeople shuffled in their seats. He was presenting a 10-hour verified training course on agents' obligations under the Real Estate Agents Act. The topic and focus was: Professional competence and ethics.

It was the best two days of professional training I've attended for many years. The Act and the Real Estate Agents Authority (REAA) are to be commended. Our legislation is world leading in attempting to elevate the professionalism of our industry. However, it's fighting a losing battle. Simply because agents are stuck in a primal conflict between two powerful but opposing forces. E*thics* versus *survival*.

Ethics is about the higher good, doing what is morally right. In a professional capacity, it's about our *duty of care* to you, our clients. This is called a *fiduciary* duty. It means we have an obligation to act at all times in your best interests. It's no different from the relationship between a doctor and patient, or a solicitor and client. It covers such things as confidentiality, transparency, disclosure and removing conflicts of interest.

Ethics is also a higher calling. As humans we inherently want to do the right thing. We gain a sense of pride and satisfaction from doing so. It helps us feel good about ourselves so we can sleep well at night, knowing we are making a positive contribution to those we serve and the world in general. I personally believe that most real estate agents want to be ethical. They genuinely want to do the right thing by you, their client.

But upon leaving the two days of training on professionalism and ethics, those salespeople go back to their offices. Back to the commission-only environment. They go back to sales training (prospecting, scripts, dialogues, and manipulative closing techniques); back to being taught about profile and self-promotion. They go back to a competitive environment where they only *eat what they catch*; back to the forces of survival.

COMMON SENSE TRUTH #4

Hungry creates a conflict of interest

Is your agent *hungry* enough? That's a good thing right? You want them to be hungry for the sale, don't you? At least that's the thinking served up by the commission-only industry: that it's somehow better for you if the agent is hungry for their commission. They'll supposedly work harder, chase more and be more persuasive to get the deal. Otherwise they get nothing. They starve. Making them more motivated.

Granted, survival is indeed a powerful motivator. In fact it's one of our strongest. A basic human instinct. Put in a situation between doing the right thing by somebody else versus ensuring our own survival? During Hurricane Katrina, in the USA, the world saw police officers looting shops to provide for their families. Was it ethical or moral for those officers to "Steal"? No! But could they rationalise and justify it in their head? Sure! So they did it… they were motivated by their survival instinct.

So is survival the motivation you want driving those acting on your behalf? Does it lead to your best interests being served?

Based on my experience, I think not. I've felt and seen the what the thirst for commission creates. I've seen salespeople (supposedly on the same team) fighting amongst themselves for scraps. I've sat through the

5

sales training, the scripts and closing techniques taught to get a deal. In order to feed their families, I've seen good people do things that go against their true character - myself included. Sadly, I've seen the clients' best interests shoved aside, stripping them of tens of thousands of dollars, while the salesperson still pocketed the commission.

This is the core of the issue. It's why I'm putting forth a voice of reason and calling for common sense thinking. It's why I'm encouraging you, and agents, to turn your back on the sales culture and help forge a new approach.

I mean, think about it... To suggest that 'adding a commission' to the equation is some how a motivator to get your agent to work harder in your best interest... Is as ridiculous as saying, it'll all be ok, when you put yourself between a steak and a hungry tiger.

Further, the industry's implication that those who don't work on commission-only are less motivated to work on your behalf, is insulting. Some would say offensive, to the every day heroes and respected professions, working hard to make a difference in our community.

Does a fireman need to be hungry in order to save lives? Does a doctor need to be hungry to make the best diagnosis for his patient? Does a lawyer need to be hungry in order to expertly defend her client? And you? Do you need to be motivated by survival in order to be the best version of yourself? To serve others? I hope not.

And tell me. Could you trust your doctor's prescription if he was hungry for a commission from the drug companies? What would happen if firemen only got a commission for putting out a fire?

This is why respected professions do not work on a commission-only sales model. They understand that being hungry creates a conflict between their clients' best interests and their own survival. A commission-only basis would erode the foundation of the relationship between themselves and their client: TRUST.

So what does motivate the best and highest-performing professionals? It's certainly not survival. It's a very different and much higher level of motivation, driven from a sense of pride in being the best at what they do, and a sense of duty to protect those they serve. It's that feeling of real accomplishment knowing they make a difference in their clients' lives.

Ask yourself: which type of motivation do you want driving the agent helping you sell, what is often, your largest asset?

COMMON SENSE TRUTH #5
If it quacks like a duck

The Duck Test is a humorous form of common sense reasoning for situations where something is not what it appears to be. It implies that you can identify an unknown subject by observing its habitual characteristics, and goes like this: *If it looks like a duck, swims like a duck, and quacks like a duck, then it probably is a duck.*

In real estate most salespeople, call themselves a 'consultant', or more specifically, 'sales consultant'. But what exactly is a sales consultant? It's clearly an oxymoron – they are either a *salesperson* or a *consultant*. They are either *selling you* on something (convincing, persuading, closing), or *consulting* with you (advising, serving, protecting, representing). It's one or the other.

Look closer at the term *sales consultant*. The second word is added to put you at ease, to make you drop your guard. It implies they are there to consult with you. So that agent, sitting at your kitchen table, trying to list your home, what are they really? Consultant or Salesperson?

Here are two ways to apply the Duck Test:

Choice: Do they offer a range of strategies, services and fee structures that can be tailored to best fit your needs? Or are they pushing a one-size-fits-all approach?

Remuneration: Are you engaging them for their expertise, counsel and services? Or do they only take a contingent commission? (Contingent meaning *dependent* upon something).

In real estate it's dependent upon you choosing to sell. Certainly a good agent can influence the transaction. They can help maximise your net profit and protect you from fundamental mistakes, but they cannot *control* the final outcome. Only you can, by accepting an offer on the table. Since you are the key decision maker, the focus becomes influencing you to do what triggers the commission.

Think of your Doctor for example. She is a consultant. Not only sworn to serve and protect, but paid for her specialist knowledge and advice. Her income is not dependent upon your decision to take her suggested prescription or not.

But what if she changed to a contingent commission model - meaning she only got paid if you chose to actually take it? All of a sudden her livelihood would become linked to how many patients she can convince to pop those pills. She'd effectively become a drug salesperson. In which case you may question the integrity of her advice. And who knows, maybe she would start calling herself a 'Sales Doctor'

So don't be fooled. Regardless of what real estate agents call themselves, traditionally they are not a *consultant*. They're a *commission-only salesperson*. Recognise that fact and understand how it affects the advice they offer you.

CHAPTER TWO

MYTH BUSTERS

COMMON SENSE TRUTH #6
Agents don't sell houses

This may initially seem counter-intuitive. After all isn't that what you pay the big commission for, to sell your house?

By *sell* I mean persuade, convince, talk a buyer into buying your property. Many believe this is what real estate salespeople do. Nothing could be further from the truth. This myth is one of the false beliefs keeping you stuck with the way the industry is.

Remember when you bought the home you're in now. You'd probably been keeping an eye on the market for some time and inspected a number of properties. Some you wouldn't have bothered looking at, because they simply didn't match your requirements. Others, upon entering, you knew immediately weren't for you. You may have found several you liked, but they weren't quite right.

While you were actively searching, you met plenty of different agents, many of whom you never spoke to again as they didn't have the right home for you on their books.

Finally, one day, you came across the right one. Who knows how you found it – online, in the newspaper, on Facebook, saw the sign, were told about it by an agent? Once found, you arranged to have a look. There was a connection. It felt right… *this is the one.*

Maybe you went back for a second look, called the bank to check your finances and did as much homework as possible before trying to buy it. Or maybe you decided to make an offer on the spot.

The point is: once your offer was accepted, the salesperson went back to their office beating their chest about how they *SOLD* you a home. But did you buy it because the salesperson talked you into it? Or because you wanted to buy it? If it had been a different salesperson at the open home – surely you'd still have wanted to buy it?

If I took you to a property that didn't suit your needs or feel right, would it matter how much of a smooth-talking salesperson I was? Am I going to *persuade* you to buy a home you simply don't like or want?

Sure, when you bought, the agent may have been helpful and informative. Maybe they negotiated hard for their client (the seller), or not. But the fact remains, they didn't *sell* you a home – you *bought* a home.

Agents don't sell houses. Buyers buy houses. What agents do is facilitate the process. This begs the question: **what is the real sales job in real estate?**

COMMON SENSE TRUTH #7

The sales job in real estate is convincing you to sell

Most consumers believe that real estate agents are focused on *selling* your property, on finding and persuading buyers to buy your property. It's logical to expect most of an agent's time and effort would be focused on this task. But it's not.

The main focus is on getting your property for sale. Most of an agent's training, time and effort is focused on finding potential sellers and persuading them to put their property on the market. Once listed, the focus shifts to persuading you do what triggers the commission.

Put another way: The first sale is winning your listing. The second sale is getting your price expectations right, and the third sale is closing for your acceptance of an offer.

Pick up any typical industry training manual. Go online and look at the sales videos and seminar topics from the industry gurus. Ask anyone who's worked in the industry. Be a fly on the wall in the majority of real estate offices anywhere in the world, and you will see this is a fact: **The sales job in real estate is not convincing buyers to buy, it's convincing you to sell.**

Will you walk into my parlour? said the Spider to the Fly...

Are the opening words of a poem by Mary Howitt, published in 1829. The story tells of a cunning Spider who ensnares a naïve Fly through the use of seduction and flattery. It's a cautionary tale against those who use flattery and charm to disguise their true intentions.

There are many ploys the real estate industry uses to try to entice you into listing with them instead of their competition. Maybe you've seen the 'Home Sale Guarantee', along the lines of *'If we can't sell your home in three months then we'll halve our fee'*, or similar.

As you now know, the only person that ultimately decides if your home sells or not, is you. So how can they possibly make such a guarantee?

Another one you see regularly, is offering to put you into a prize draw: *List with us and you could win a holiday, or a car...*

These do nothing to help increase your selling price or reduce your selling costs. They do not protect your interests or help you achieve a superior result when selling your property. They are simply gimmicks designed to lure you into listing.

Of the many ways the industry baits you, the most common that sellers go for is the FREE Market Appraisal.

A FREE Market Appraisal is a sales pitch

Offering free market appraisals is a ploy to get in your door, to give salespeople the opportunity to *sell* you on the benefits of listing with them. It's the start of a real estate salesperson's *Sales Funnel*. Remember that YOU (as a potential seller) are the first sales target for real estate agents.

So when you call a typical agent and ask for a free market appraisal, thinking you are getting a free and useful service that will help you budget your next move, you are actually inviting a salesperson into your home to give you a sales pitch. Technically, this could be called *Bait and Switch*, the *bait* being the Free Appraisal and the *switch* being the real reason they are there – to win your listing.

Consider how many people go about inviting an agent into their home: *Who shall we call in for an appraisal?… How about the agent dealing with the property we are interested in buying, and the one that put a flyer in our letter box last week. Also, Jill's friend Jo has just got into real estate; she seems nice, I'd like to give her a chance too.*

What they really need is genuine advice about the current value of their home, as a basis for sound decision making for their family's future. Yet look at how they selected who they invited to 'advise' them. Many think that all agents are the same or that anyone will do, giving little thought as to the agent's credentials, qualifications or experience. They don't ask themselves if the agent actually knows what he or she is doing. For instance... what is the agent's 'Market Appraisal Accuracy Rate': what price did their last 50 clients actually achieve compared to their upfront appraisal range?

Most salespeople have had very little (if any) formal training on valuation principles. Most training is sales based – how to overcome your objections, sales scripts and closes to get your listing.
The skill set needed to accurately value your property is very different to that needed to persuade you to list with them. The first requires analytical skills, deep knowledge of what affects value, and

experience interpreting the local market dynamics. The second is mostly about being liked, and about getting you to feel good about them.

Consider this: even if they do know what they are doing and have the skills to value your property, and if they do put in the necessary research and effort to ensure their appraisal is accurate, can you rely on their advice?

Unlike a, independant Valuer, a commission-only salesperson will only be compensated for their work and advice *IF* you choose to sell your property with them.

They learn quickly that you are likely to have an inflated opinion of the value of your own home. This is natural. It's called the Endowment Effect: As humans we place an unrealistically high value on our own possessions, especially those we are emotionally attached to.

They also learn that people often *shoot the messenger* and instead list their property with those who *tell them what they want to hear*. So if the salesperson tells you the truth about the likely sale price of your home – they greatly decrease their chances winning your listing.

Let's say you call in several agents to give you a 'quote'. Your home is really worth around $300,000 but because of the Endowment Effect you are hoping for $320,000. Agent 'A' does their homework and tells you the truth. Agent 'B' seems more enthusiastic, and tells you what you want to hear… *I've got buyers that I think will pay you $320,000.*

Who do you want to believe? The higher one of course. And, because deep down you don't trust real estate agents, you probably think agent 'A' was just talking low to try to get a quick easy commission.

Therefore, by asking a commission-only salesperson for a FREE Market Appraisal, you are putting them in a difficult position.

On one hand, if they really cared for your financial wellbeing, they would encourage you to budget conservatively. Any budget advisor worth their salt, will advise you that most people make the mistake of overestimating their potential income (sale price) and underestimating their expenses (selling costs). They end up a lot worse off financially than they planned. The wise thing to do is budget conservatively on your projected income and overestimate your likely expenses. That way you should be financially safe. If your property is most likely to sell around $300,000, it's in your best interests to budget on getting $300,000 or slightly less.

Yet a salesperson has a dilemma – give you the right advice and risk not getting the chance to sell your property (thus no commission) or tell you what you want to hear. For a moment, put yourself in their shoes – which would have higher priority – your clients' financial wellbeing or your family's survival?

This is not to say that commission-only salespeople are bad people. Most genuinely care about their clients. What I am saying is that the commission-only model puts them in this conflicted position. As John C. Maxwell (New York Times bestselling author) puts it in his book *There's no such thing as business ethics* :

'If I believe that I have only two choices: (1) to win by doing whatever it takes, even if it's unethical; or (2) to have ethics and lose - I'm faced with a real moral dilemma. Few people set out with the desire to be dishonest, but nobody wants to lose.'

A tip: don't muddy the waters. Often, people get an appraisal because they need to know what their property is worth *before* they can decide whether or not they should put it on the market.

In this case there are two separate and fundamentally different questions to be answered. The first is:

How much is my property likely to sell for?

Here you need reliable and unbiased advice so you can safely budget. Those advising must not only know what they are doing when it comes to valuing, but also be completely straight up and honest with you. Then, and only then, can you decide if you should be trying to sell. If the answer is yes, then the next question is:

What is the best way to approach the selling process, so that we maximise our profit?

This is about strategy (your approach to the market), presentation, marketing, negotiation skills, creating multiple offers, extracting a premium from the market if possible, and of course minimising your selling costs. By getting a Free Market Appraisal from a commission-only salesperson, you are mixing these steps together. You are muddying the waters. Avoid this by keeping them separate.

When budgeting and assessing how much your property is likely to sell for – either get an Independent Registered Valuation or an Unbiased Market Appraisal. The latter can be sought from an experienced agent who has an excellent Appraisal Accuracy Rate and engage them, as you would a valuer, to give you unbiased advice. So instead of only paying them if you choose to sell (like a Free Market Appraisal), offer to pay them a fair fee (for their time, experience and expertise) to give you good advice.

This way, there is no *sales pitch* involved. There is no longer a *conflict of interest*. The agent can give you the same advice as they would a family member, without fear of working for nothing.

Should you decide, based on the agent's advice, that it's not in your best interest to sell, then the agent is still rewarded for helping you come to that decision. Both your and the agent's best interests are aligned. The waters are not muddied.

Then, if you decide to sell, interview agents for the job of putting your property to market and maximising your net profit from the sale.

You are not asking:

How much can you sell my house for?

You are asking:

How will you go about maximising my sale price and minimising my selling costs?... Or
What strategies do you advise for extracting a premium price from the market, and how will you charge for that service?

This is a very different discussion.

Value is an opinion

While studying for a valuation degree we were taught to analyse value in a logical way – looking at tangible and measurable things like floor area, land size, age, and the like, then comparing with similar recently-sold properties in the immediate location. We were taught to be objective, to remove emotion from the equation. For a valuer this is necessary. If challenged, they must be able to stand up in court and prove their case. They must be able to logically justify how they arrived at their stated value.

After graduating, instead of becoming a Registered Valuer, I chose to enter the real estate industry. It didn't take long to realise that while logical analysis has an important place for budgeting purposes, even a Registered Valuation is just an educated stab in the dark. Why? Because 'value' is not logical, it's an *opinion*.

What something is worth to you can be completely different from its worth to the next person – especially for property, or things that hold an emotional connection.

This is demonstrated when more than one buyer wants to buy the same property at the same time. In these situations each buyer is required to put their best offer forward, or risk missing out. We very rarely see two offers of exactly the same price, and even rarer with the same price and conditions. Sometimes they are close, but more often than not there are large variations. Even in my small market, where the median price is currently around $320,000, I've seen differences between offers of more than $50,000. (As an aside, this is why I seldom recommend clients sell by Public Auction.)

This reinforces the fact that value is a matter of opinion when selling your home. Nobody can tell you exactly what your property will sell for in advance. Nobody has a crystal ball.

Ultimately, there are only two opinions that matter: Yours as the seller, and that of the best buyer. As we will discuss shortly, finding that best buyer has nothing to with your agent's opinion (what they say to win your listing). It's about getting your strategy and process right by implementing a proven and documented approach that consistently creates a superior result.

CHAPTER THREE

SOME TRUTHS ABOUT ADVERTISING AND BUYERS

You can't sell a secret

Is a line often spoken by agents. It lays the premise that in order to sell you must advertise your property, which on the surface seems to make sense, right? I'm not saying that *smart marketing* isn't an important tool to attract buyers, it is. But the maxim, *You can't sell a secret,* is rubbish.

Of course you can sell a secret. Secrets sell all the time. Every day, millions of secrets are sold worldwide, from national security secrets to secret formula diets.

COMMON SENSE TRUTH #10
Secrets are worth more

Reflect on this: what is worth more? What commands a higher value – common knowledge - a commodity which everybody can have, or a secret - which is something special and exclusive? It's no contest, a secret wins hands-down. There are psychological reasons why this is so, like wanting what we can't have, and feeling special because we have something others don't. There's no disputing humans will jump through hoops to pay a premium for a secret. That's why secrets are one of the secrets smart marketers use to get premium prices for their products and services.

So why would a commission-only salesperson suggest *You can't sell a secret*? Several reasons come to mind. Either:

They believe it. It's what they've been taught. Unfortunately this indicates they have never studied smart marketing. Which is concerning. You want them to know how to create a premium for their client's product (your property).

Or, they are selling you the need for advertising.

In the commission-only sales culture, the recommended way for an individual salesperson to increase their listings is to maximise their personal 'profile'. The more advertising they have out there, showing their name and photo, the more successful they will appear and therefore attract more sellers like you. This is driven from the top down. The Brand or Franchise encourages its salespeople to advertise more because they also want their logo on as much advertising as possible. They want to have the most pages in the local property rag. For them, the name of the game is looking the biggest.

COMMON SENSE TRUTH #11

Advertising does not add value to your home

If you accept the *you can't sell a secret* line, then you are ripe for the up-sell. There are two forms of advertising up-sell. Firstly bigger adverts – a half page or full page in print media or upgrading to a feature on the internet portals. Secondly, more advertising – doubling or tripling the same advertisement in multiple publications.

Just like *You can't sell a secret*, the suggestions encouraging you to advertise BIGGER and MORE are absurd. Agents claim that bigger and more advertising will get you more buyers and a better price. There is absolutely no evidence to suggest that a bigger advertisement adds any value whatsoever to your property. As if a buyer would think to themselves ... *"those sellers had a full page advert – I'd better offer them another $10,000!"*

Also nonsense is the premise that the number of buyers in the market is linked to the amount of advertising. Doubling the advertising won't somehow magically double the number of buyers.

Informed sellers understand that there are only so many genuine buyers in the market at any point in time. This is affected mainly by economic factors. Advertising has nothing to do with it. If it did, then why is it that over the last 30 years the amount of real estate advertising has almost tripled, yet the number of sales being made is the about the same?

In my local market you have the choice of three different print publications. Research tells us that genuine buyers are keeping an eye on all three. Therefore as long as you advertise in one of them, they will find your property.

Of course all those pages of unnecessary advertising – with the agents' photos and company branding all over it – certainly make them look good. The problem is: it's very expensive. Who do you think is ultimately paying?

An interesting fact to ponder is that at least 85% of buyers' enquiries are now made via the internet, yet as a whole the industry is still spending 85% of the marketing funds on expensive and less effective print media.

To reiterate, I am not saying that *smart marketing* isn't an important part of attracting buyers. However there is a balance between attracting buyers and damaging your value. There is a point where continuing to advertise your property works against your best interests.

COMMON SENSE TRUTH #12
Advertising can damage your value

Have you ever seen a property wallowing on the market, being advertised week-in, week-out – but not selling? What does it make you think about the property? The two most common replies are:
What's wrong with it? and *It must be overpriced.* Although both of these may be true, they could also be false. The point being, true or false, they are both negative perceptions about your property – created by it being over-exposed to the market.

It may be good for the agent's profile to hammer your property, but both of those resulting negative perceptions can do massive damage to its perceived value, and at the same time help keep traditional commissions so inefficiently high.

As we will discuss in Part Three – if your property is not selling or you need to hang out for a price above the current market, there are much smarter strategies that not only keep your home special, but also reduce your selling costs to a minimum, which in turn increases your net profit
.

Which agent has the most buyers?

This is a question many sellers ponder, understandably, when selecting an agent. It may seem that some agents will have more buyers than others. Unfortunately this misconception is a trap.

Remember common sense truth #7: The *sales job* in real estate is convincing you to sell.

To persuade you to list with them over other agents, they may claim they have more buyers. You've probably heard the lines...

> *We've got the biggest team...We do the most advertising...We sell more in your price bracket, neighbourhood ...*

As a sales tactic, it's designed to trigger the fear of missing out. They imply that if you don't list your property with them, you'll lose good buyers. Let's clear up this falsehood with a quiz:

Which agent has the most buyers for your property? The one:

    a. With the largest pack of salespeople?
    b. That does the most advertising?
    c. Belonging to a national brand?
    d. Selling more in your area/price range?
    e. None of the above?

The honest answer is: None of the above.

Think about this: let's say you have a favourite real estate agent, maybe a friend or family member you'd really like to buy through. The problem is, they don't have every home on their books, so you still need to look at what other agents have. Your friend is trying really hard but just hasn't come up with the right place. In the meantime, it comes onto the market with a different agent. It looks perfect for your family, is in the ideal location and it's within your budget. Are you going ignore it? Are you going to walk away from your ideal home just because it's not listed with your favourite agent? Not likely. You see, as a buyer, finding the right home is more important than who you happen to buy it through.

COMMON SENSE TRUTH #13

Buyers are attracted to your property, not the agent

Not so long ago, an agent phoned one of my clients claiming he *had a buyer for her property*. She explained that I was her agent and suggested he give me a call. His reply, *No I don't share my buyers*, putting the fear of missing out onto her.

Long story short, within 48 hours I received a call from none other than that agent's daughter, wanting to book an inspection. Yes, even his own daughter was more concerned about finding the right home than who she purchased it through.

This shows that buyers are not loyal to agents. They just want the best property they can find and don't care who you are on the market with. Any genuine buyers, looking for a property like yours, are going to view it regardless of whose sign is on the fence.

COMMON SENSE TRUTH #14

Every agent has exactly the same number of buyers

Any that claim otherwise are either blinkered or deliberately misleading you – buyers aren't kept locked away in a dungeon somewhere.

Rather than asking which agent has the most buyers it may be wiser to ask which agent do you want representing you when those buyers are negotiating to buy your property? In other words, which agent do you believe will best protect your interests and maximise how much you bank?

CHAPTER FOUR

WHAT YOU ARE REALLY PAYING FOR?

COMMON SENSE TRUTH #15
You are paying for agents to find you

Suppose there's a random knock at your door. Turns out it's Pete the plumber who is in your street today and is wondering if you need any plumbing work done. In a stroke of luck, you just happen to have a blocked drain, so engage him to fix it. He spends approximately one hour on the job. A week later you receive an invoice for plumbing services totalling five hours' work. In confusion you call the plumber and ask what the extra four hours were charged for?

I had to knock on doors for three hours before I found you. Plus, I did an hour's work for your neighbour last month who didn't pay me – so I added that to your bill also.

I doubt you would accept that from your plumber – or any other professional service provider. Yet this is exactly what is happening with the traditional real estate model.

Several years ago, real estate industry commentator Alistair Helm shared that:

Real estate agents spend over 64% of their working week prospecting for business.

To clarify, *prospecting for business* does not mean looking for buyers to buy your property, it means looking for and persuading sellers (like you), to sell their property. Alistair continued:

The productive time spent on behalf of their clients in facilitating the sale of a house represents less than 25% of their working week. Yet their income from sellers supports their full working week.

So, with the traditional real estate model, you are paying for agents to spend the majority of their time and resources finding you. This is no different from paying for the plumber to knock on other people's doors.

COMMON SENSE TRUTH #16
Commissions support more salespeople than needed

Alistair also pointed out:

There are just too many agents tripping over each other, fighting one another, stabbing each other in the back to get a listing and from there to conclude a sale and ultimately earn a commission.

Study any local market and you will find far more salespeople than needed. In my small town there are currently around 60 active salespeople chasing an average of 50 sales per month. How can that be? Surely it doesn't take 60 real estate agents to facilitate 50 transactions? No it doesn't. However, because traditional commissions are so high, 60 agents are supported by only 50 sales.

The industry perpetuates this problem. As property values rise (and therefore commissions) those commissions can support more salespeople. So the industry continues to recruit more. Why? The preached path to market share under the traditional industry model, is what many call *bums on seats*...Take on as many commission-only salespeople as possible – the more salespeople the office has, the bigger and more successful the agency will look. It's not about becoming more efficient or doing a better job for you their client. It's about being seen as the BIGGEST.

Alistair put it this way: *The Industry... want the inefficiency, they want to have agents fighting each other for listings ... The industry protects the model and the consumer pays – heavily.*

Free is bait for the uninformed

A few months back I came across an excellent article on stuff.co.nz warning consumers of the hidden costs and dangers of *Interest-free finance deals*. You know, the ones offered by the retail industry to encourage more of us to buy their products: *36 Months Interest Free* or *Pay nothing for 12 months* on products like a new washing machine, TV, or the latest must-have gizmo.

The writer pointed out that while *Interest-free deals can be appealing if you don't have the funds*, they can also be a trap and a lot more expensive than you think.

Personally I found the readers' comments on the article most telling: *The interest is always getting paid by someone. Either in fees or inflated rrp's. Anyone who thinks a shop is nice and doing them a deal is a fool. Nothing is free ever.*

And this: *These deals are toxic and are aimed at the desperate and uninformed amongst us.* Sad but true. It's often the desperate or uninformed who seem to take such bait.

It's similar to the way the real estate industry encourages more of you to put your property on the market. It's called *No Sale - No Fee* and is pitched along the lines of:

List your property with us… we'll give you free advertising etc… and you don't have to pay anything, unless we sell it for the price you want. There's no risk listing with us —you've got nothing to lose … just sign this paperwork and we'll get underway.

As you can see, it's designed to put you at ease. And on the surface it seems like a good deal. If you choose not to accept what the best buyer will currently pay for your property, or change your mind and decide not to sell at all, then offering your property *for sale* will cost you *nothing*. But look at the bigger picture – not only does this create a conflict of interest…

There is no such thing as a free lunch

Any business that gives away time, resources or products to some people must recover it back from others.

Let's say you manufacture a gizmo that costs $1,000 each to produce. As a special promotion, you offer it to 100 buyers with a *one in 3 chance to win their money back* (in other words 33 will be given away for free). How much would you have to charge the other 67 buyers in order to cover your production costs? *Answer*: **$1,492**.

The paying buyers would need to stump up a whopping 49% extra to subsidise the ones who got it for free. And that's just to break even, let alone make some profit.

This is what's happening every day in the real estate industry. The reality is: **the fees from clients who do sell need to be high enough to cover the losses incurred from the clients who don't.**

Genuine sellers subsidise the non-sellers

Here are the facts: traditionally around 70% of people who put their property on the market actually sell. Why should they have to use a model that favours the 30% of people who, for whatever reason, ultimately decide not to sell and thus pay nothing for the work done on their behalf?

At least with the retail industry you have the choice to avoid the interest-free schemes by paying on the spot. With the traditional real estate industry you are given no such choice, it's the one-size-fits-all commission-only scheme or nothing.

Commission removes your ability to reduce costs

The industry wants you to believe that it's all about getting you the highest price. Agents claim they will get you a better price than the next agent and spout all the reasons why... *we're the biggest, do the most advertising...*

Most of the reasons they give don't in fact ensure you get the best price at all (more on that soon).

The main point is this: you are being misdirected. Certainly, getting the highest price possible is important and it's vital you have an agent working for you that has the skills and a proven approach to do so. However, what is more important? The eventual sale price or how much you net after expenses? Obviously the latter. But with commission-only, because it's a percentage of your sale price, your fees cannot be reduced, even if your property sells in a day.

The industry doesn't want you to focus on your net price, because you may then question the true costs of selling. The best way to illustrate how all this works, is to tell you a story...

A Tale of Four Home Sellers...

Once upon a time four home sellers put their properties on the market. Apart from going it alone and trying to sell privately, they had no real choice other than to list with traditional real estate agents on a No Sale – No Fee commission-only basis. The going rate in town was $500 plus 3% of their sale price, plus GST.

Ken took responsibility for his sale. He had a definite plan and knew that he was in control of his property selling or not. He understood his actions and decisions would ultimately dictate the outcome. He worked hard to present his property at its best and had realistic price expectations. He put a smart strategy in place and targeted achieving a sale in the first two weeks (which, by the way, is when you will get the most buyer interest). It worked a treat. He received multiple offers and sold for a premium of $400,000. He was a dream client. His agent outlaid only $800 in marketing expenses and did six hours of direct work on Ken's behalf. Although Ken was happy with the quick sale, he was left with a sour taste in his mouth. He felt the **$14,375** in commission they had to pay was a lot, considering how little work was involved for the agent.

Clare on the other hand, wanted to move but accepted no responsibility for the sale of her property. She put little effort into presenting it well and set an unrealistic asking price. She turned down a good early offer but after three months' of constant advertising, her property had become stale. She finally accepted a sale at $400,000. The agent outlaid $1,600 in marketing expenses and did 12 hours of direct work. Clare paid exactly the same **$14,375** in commission, as Ken.

Bob was much like Ken but lived on the other side of town. His property was perfectly presented and realistically priced. In under two weeks he had multiple offers driving the price up to more than expected. He was thrilled to sell for $200,000. The agent did exactly the same amount of work as for Ken ($800 in marketing expenses and 6 hours of direct work). However Bob only paid **$7,475** in commission.

Then there was Larry. He didn't really need to sell but thought he'd throw it on the market for a silly price. Thinking it would make them work harder, he listed it with two different agents. It wallowed on the market for six months. In that time, Larry turned down three fair offers before finally taking it off the market. He told all his friends the agents were *hopeless* as *they couldn't sell his house*. Between the two of them, the agents spent $5,000 on advertising and did thirty hours of direct work. Larry paid **nothing**.

What's wrong with this story?

Ken did everything right. He made his agent's job a lot easier and less expensive – yet he still paid the same fee as Clare, who needed twice as much work. And, just because his property was worth more, he had to pay twice as much as Bob, across town, whose sale took exactly the same amount of effort and outgoing costs for the agent. Of course all of them (Ken, Clare, and Bob) were subsidising Larry.

It doesn't seem right, but that's the way the system works. It's broken. It rewards the few people who take time and resources but ultimately choose not to sell, and it punishes the majority of genuine clients who do everything in their power to make the selling process easier.

It doesn't have to be this way. In Part Three we will look at a simple solution that's fairer, more transparent and much more efficient for the genuine sellers.

CHAPTER FIVE

THE TRUTH ABOUT REAL ESTATE NEGOTIATIONS

COMMON SENSE TRUTH #21

The traditional style of negotiating helps buyers to get your property for less

According to real estate consumer advocate and author Neil Jenman:

The biggest "COST" with most agents is not commission, it's their INCOMPETENCE at not knowing how to negotiate – thereby "UNDERSELLING" homes!

And frankly... I agree.

All agents say they'll negotiate the *best price*. However I've found that the typical real estate industry style of negotiating helps the buyer get your property for *less* than they were prepared to pay – thus underselling your property. Again, the best way to demonstrate this to you is with a true story:

If only they knew

"You have to tell people about this. They have a right to know". Liz was talking about warning you, everyday sellers who don't realise what is going on.

Unfortunately, *if only they knew* is a phrase often expressed in our office, sometimes with just a sigh and shake of the head. Other times we get angry. We hate seeing people ripped off. Even when they are not one of our clients. Stories like this strengthen our resolve to lead positive change.

This case relates directly to two of our core purposes – protecting you from costly mistakes and maximising how much you bank. In order to bank the most profit, you must first raise your sale price as high as possible. Achieving that requires the competent execution of five key steps. One of those, is the *negotiation*, that happens between the buyer making an offer and the final terms being agreed upon.

Adam had been helping Bill and Sue (names changed) sell their property before finding one more suitable for their retirement. Although not quite officially sold, theirs was under contract and very close to being unconditional. So they were in a strong position to secure their next home. They knew exactly how much they had in their hand and could make a clean offer on something else.

They found the one they wanted. It was listed with a traditional agent for $399,000. Before making an offer to the other agent, they spoke to Adam on our team for some guidance. Instinctively his first question was *How much will you pay, if needed?*. $395,000 was their walk-away price. (Keep this in mind as you read on).

Knowing the style of negotiating most salespeople employ, Adam gave them some inside tips on how to possibly turn that to their advantage (as buyers). You'll be amazed at the outcome.

They made an opening offer to the seller's agent of $380,000. She said she *didn't think her clients would take that* – but without even asking for more, went off to find out. A short time later she arrived back with a counter offer from the sellers of $390,000. So at this point they were already $5,000 under what Bill and Sue would've paid.

You can probably guess how it goes from here... Bill & Sue counter-offered back to the sellers at $385,000. To their delight the sellers accepted.

As buyers, Bill & Sue were thrilled. They got the home for $10,000 less than they were prepared to pay. Interestingly they also commented to Adam about how nice the seller's agent was … *So helpful and easy to deal with.* She was indeed great for them as buyers… not so for her client, the seller.

And that's what riles me about this common scenario. Those sellers don't have any inkling of what just happened to them – that their agent just burned $10,000 of their equity. On top of that they probably paid her a traditional $12,000–$15,000 commission for the privilege. That was one very costly selling exercise.

Although I get angry that agents can be so negligent of their duties to their client, I don't believe it's 100% their fault. Most real estate salespeople have never had any real negotiation training other than being taught how to negotiate to secure a deal. But there is a big difference between that and negotiating to find the buyers' highest price.

Most agents just do what this industry teaches and encourages them to do. In this case, the agent is probably unaware that her style of negotiating cost her clients $10,000.

So, I blame the industry – the Commission-only business model and the Sales Culture that drives it. That is where these problems begin.

It teaches its agents to be Salespeople. It encourages a style of negotiating which is designed to get a deal as quickly as possible – to get a commission – not the best price for the seller. It focuses on the lowest figure the seller will take instead of the most the buyer will pay. It's often about persuading the seller to accept the buyer's low offer, rather than making sure the buyer is offering their best.

If only they knew.

PART TWO
The Common Sense Solution

"We cannot solve our problems
with the same thinking we used
when we created them."

Albert Einstein

REAL ESTATE RESTATED

Enough is enough. I could provide example after example of how the Commission-only model and sales culture work against you. But I hope by now you are seeing the bigger picture.

I think we both deserve better. I can see an industry that's more professional, puts your interests above its own and adds genuine value to those it serves – an industry you can trust and that agents can be truly proud to be a part of.

Many have told me I'm a dreamer, that I was fooling myself, that it couldn't be done. *The industry will never change*, they said. Yes they are right – it will never change while everyone continues to accept the way it works. Albert Einstein coined it brilliantly: *We cannot solve our problems with the same thinking we used when we created them.*

So we asked ourselves – what if we start with a clean sheet and redesign the industry for today's world – how would it look? How can we raise professionalism and at the same time create more value for our clients?

The solution is amazingly simple, yet requires us to think differently. It requires us to reject the sales culture and the problems it creates. It requires us to restate what this industry is all about.

Traditionally real estate is seen as a *Sales Industry*. And as you can now see, it's this model, the Commission-only and the sales culture that is the root cause of the problems. What if we changed that? Instead of acting like a *Sales Industry*, what if we restated real estate to be a *Professional*

Service Industry? Just as all respected professions work, where they protect and serve, and the fees transparently reflect the actual work carried out on each individual client's behalf?

It is said, *you get what you expect*. When you, as a home seller, see real estate as a *Professional Service*, you expect us to act accordingly. You demand transparency, high standards of professionalism, a choice of services and fair fees. When, we as agents see ourselves as *Professional Service Providers*, then we also act accordingly. It becomes a self-fulfilling prophecy.

The really exciting thing is that this is no longer just a theory. It is now tested and proven beyond doubt. As of writing, 161 pioneering clients have entrusted us to implement the Common Sense Approach on their behalf. Combined, they have netted $756,328 more than they would have with the traditional commission-only model. That is an average of around $4,700 more in each of their pockets. (And that's based on our average local sale price of around $330,000 - so imagine the added equity sellers in higher valued markets will be gaining).

But that's not all. We are also finding the relationships with our clients are on a much higher level. We are working together for a common goal – to maximise their net gains after expenses. Their best interests and ours are now aligned.

Many of our clients are not only giving us amazing written references, but also enthusiastically spreading the word, recommending us to their friends and families. Their support and encouragement has been phenomenal – like nothing I've ever seen in over 25 years in this industry.

Of course this has enabled us to stay more efficient, and to keep focused on just working for our clients. We no longer need to spend most of our time and effort *prospecting*, nor lose time, effort and money working for people like 'Larry' (*A Tale of Four Home Sellers*). In turn this means we don't need to inflate the fees for our genuine clients.

Overall, this has created what's called a *Positive Feedback Loop*. In a nutshell, because the 'Professional Service' model is creating consistently superior results for our clients, they in turn are spreading the message and helping to attract more clients... which then enables us to keep focused on helping more clients … and so the positive loop continues. It's a breakthrough – a real-world win/win.

Breakthrough vs Discount.

Some people – when they see the extra net profits the Common Sense Approach is achieving for clients – think there must be a catch. Some even assume that we are just *discounting* the traditional way. But we are not.

There is a massive difference between a discount and a breakthrough. Invariably, discounting leads to inferior products and services. Hence the saying *pay peanuts – get monkeys*.

When it comes to real estate, discounting the traditional commission-only model does nothing but exaggerate the rotten core – leading to poorer services and even more questionable ethics.

In contrast, in the book *Platform Revolution*, the authors tell the story of steel production during the industrial era. A new process of blowing air through molten slag was discovered. It removed impurities and cut production costs from £40 to £7 per ton. That was a breakthrough. It not only reduced costs but also improved quality – forever changing the steel industry.

In a similar way, the Common Sense Approach is not playing around with an already broken model. It is not a 'discount'. It is a new model, a more efficient process that has changed the game. It's a breakthrough that is helping clients receive higher levels of professionalism and more in their pockets.

Before I outline the key steps to implement 'The Common Sense Approach to Sell Real Estate', and especially if you are considering engaging an agent certified in this approach, then it's important for you to understand our core values. These are the beliefs that guide our actions and enable the approach to work. They are the solid foundation upon which the approach is built.

We Protect

In our eyes, you are a client to be protected, not a prospect to be stalked. Nor a lead to be converted nor a listing target to be closed. Our heroes, the professions we admire, are the ones who are sworn to protect and serve - nurses, doctors, lawyers, firemen, paramedics, teachers, police, the armed forces and so on. Theirs is the type of culture we aspire to. So first and foremost, we are here to protect you from fundamental mistakes and traps. Unfortunately many of them are laid by the traditional real estate industry. That's why I wrote this book, to open your eyes. The best protection is to avoid them in the first place.

We Question

Questions are at the heart of professional consulting. Each and every one of you have unique circumstances, a unique property and differing needs that deserve tailored solutions. Just as a doctor must first question before diagnosing and prescribing, we also must fully understand your situation, needs and goals before we can recommend your best course of action. We believe that prescription without diagnosis is malpractice. We also question the status quo, the way our industry traditionally works. We refuse to be dictated to by the establishment. Just because they've always done it that way doesn't mean it's the best way. We believe in innovation, in improvement, in finding and developing better and more efficient ways for you, our clients.

We Advise

You engage us to use our specialist knowledge and experience to your advantage. This points to a primary difference between a sales culture and a professional consultative one. A salesperson's function is to persuade, convince, coax you into doing what enables them to reach their targets and get a commission. Their agenda is to influence your decisions in their favour. As a professional consultant, our agenda is to advise, recommend, coach and guide, so you can make informed decisions for yourself and your family.

We Serve

Without you to serve, we wouldn't exist. Once we fully understand your personal situation and have made recommendations as to your best course of action, our role is to then act on your behalf. We follow through on your decisions and instructions to the best of our ability, at all times *serving* your interests.

We Create Value

You engage us to put more in your pocket than you would have had without us. Whether you need full-service sale of your home, assistance negotiating with a private buyer, or just some one-off professional advice, our function is to act and advise in the most efficient way possible for you. Being known to help you net more is the reputation we've worked hard to earn and are passionate about keeping. So if we genuinely can't create value, then we will advise you so.

PART THREE

The Common Sense Approach
to sell your property.

CHAPTER SEVEN

IT STARTS WITH YOU

What do you want? It's a simple enough question, yet one many of us struggle to clearly define in many areas of our lives. When we are not clear about what we want we tend to drift along rudderless, at the mercy of the currents. Often those currents lead us in the wrong direction. Instead of working towards achieving our own goals, we can become a pawn in other peoples.

It's only luck that will get us to where we want, if we don't know where that is when we set out.. So the first step to achieving anything is to define exactly what *it* is we want to achieve.

The next challenge is figuring out *how* to achieve it. For me this has often been a stumbling block. I've had plenty of things I wanted to do, that have come to nothing because I didn't know how to do it. The inability to put a plan in place stopped the goal in its tracks. Other times I followed the wrong plan and therefore ended up in the wrong place.

A life hack, I wish I'd learned earlier, is leveraging other people's knowledge, formulas, and proven action plans. Often the best way to do something has already been discovered and documented by others. If you've never made a carrot cake, you would be wise to start with a recipe (somebody else's formula to follow that will consistently create a good cake). The best recipes are not thought up overnight, they are discovered slowly, perfected over time with trial and error, learning from successes and failures. You can either develop your own formula, or you can take advantage of other people's.

This is where trades, services and professions come from. You are choosing to pay for other people's specialist skills, knowledge and proven formulas to help you achieve what you want, rather than figuring it all out yourself.

Selling your property is no different. It's never the dominant goal (the reason why you are selling in the first place). It's a step in the overall plan. But if you don't clearly define what you want from the sale, then it's highly likely you will be lead around by the currents. You could find yourself following the wrong plan, one set by others with their own agendas. You will be at the mercy of their desired outcomes instead of being in control of your own.

So I ask again: What do you want? Why are you selling in the first place? You may be wondering why these questions are important One word: strategy.

Strategy

This is your overall approach to the market, your game plan. Are you definitely selling and want the best result in the short term? Or, will only sell *if…* you get *x* price, can secure another property, or other conditions?

This is vitally important. Your goals affect your strategy, which in turn determines your method of sale, marketing and ideal fee structure.

Let's say that you need $400,000. You don't mind how long it takes, but you simply will not sell unless you get it. This demands a different game plan than if you need a sale within a specific timeframe – where you want to net as much as possible but it must be sold by Christmas.

Firstly, you will gain the most buyer interest and have the best chance of a multiple offer (helping you achieve a premium if handled correctly) in the first two weeks of going to market. This is simply because there is a pool of ready and waiting buyers in the market at any point in time. When a new listing hits the market that pool of buyers will pounce; after that, the number drops to an occasional new buyer, drip-feeding into the market.

So here's the thing, when you launch to the market, that pool of buyers will either see the value you want, or they won't. If they do then that's great, you'll sell. If they don't, then as the seller you have two choices: you can either adjust your expectation to where the buyers are now and get on with your life, or you can wait for the market to rise to you. (In a rising market you may not have to wait long. In a falling market… who knows?). Fundamentally, regardless of what you are trying to sell, it's either a pricing game or a waiting game.

Let's say you are happy to play the *waiting game* and disclose to the agent, up front, that you will only sell if you get $400,000.

Considering Common Sense Truth #7: *The sales job in real estate is convincing you to sell*, do you think a commission-only salesperson is likely to advise you that *the price you are needing is above the current market* and risk you not listing your property with them? Or are they more likely to say: *No problem, I can get you that, I've got buyers coming out my ears, sign here?* But what happens if the current buyers don't see that value? Suddenly the previously optimistic salesperson's tune will change. His focus shifts to trying to convince you to reduce your expectations. Because he can't get a commission unless you accept the current market.

If you stay staunch and don't sway under the pressure, then that same agent will encourage you to leave it on the market for as long as it takes. They hope they can hang onto your listing long enough to fluke a sale. In the meantime they advertise intensely, which as I noted earlier, is damaging the perception of your property in the market. The longer you stay exposed the worse it looks. When that right buyer eventually does turn up, your property is perceived as a lemon and they are less likely to make a high offer.

In this situation another strategy would be to test the market for a maximum of two to three weeks…

Are there any buyers out there, right now, who see our value?.

If not, then give it rest and remove it from the market. Then in a month or six weeks' time put it back to the market… *Are there any buyers out there who see our value now?* Wash. Rinse. Repeat – until the market has risen to you.

This way, rather than wallowing on the market going stale, you are taking short sharp stabs at the market. Each time you launch, your property is like a new listing to the buyers in the market at that point in time, keeping it special and making it much more likely to generate a multiple offer – which in turn can drive your price even higher.

(In Part Five are a few comments from some of our clients. Find Anne-Marie and Bernard. This strategy worked perfectly for them).

COMMON SENSE TRUTH #22

One size does not fit all

It doesn't when it applies to your clothes. It doesn't for your medical care, or your children's education, and it certainly doesn't when it comes to selling your home.

I've never seen two clients with identical circumstances. The fact is that each of you has unique needs that deserve a tailored solution. Maybe you are best going to the market all guns blazing, targeting a sale in the first two weeks. Maybe you are better with a quieter more discreet approach. Maybe you are best to play a waiting game, keeping your property special. The point is, each overall game plan is different, and put together from a range of selling methods, smart marketing tactics, and fee structures.

At this point let's assume that you have a definite goal and selling your property is a required step to achieving it. The next thing to consider is:

What is most important to you about the sale?

I just want it SOLD so I can (insert overall reason for selling) is a common answer and it's a start. But we need to dig deeper. You can get a sale any time you like. Any traditional salesperson can get you a sale, because that's what they focus on. To them the sale, and therefore a commission' is the goal. But this is important… do you just want a sale at any cost or do you want to *net* as much as possible from the sale?

Now you are getting clearer about what you really want. If you simply don't care about maximising your net profit, then this book is of no value to you. If however you do want to maximise your net profit, the first formula to etch into your mind follows.

COMMON SENSE TRUTH #23

Net profit equals sale price minus expenses

In order to *net* the most, you must first get your sale price as high as possible while at the same time keep your selling costs as low as possible. Simple isn't it.

Agent or Private Sale?

Do you want to engage the services of a real estate professional or sell privately? Do you believe you will be better off with or without an agent?

I'm not going to try to talk you out of selling privately. Plenty of people do very well themselves, often much better than they would have with a traditional commission-only salesperson.

Sometimes a private sale is your best solution and all you may need is a little advice and guidance along the way.

We call it Private Sale Assist – maybe an Unbiased Market Appraisal to ensure you are getting a fair price, some help drafting the contract or negotiating with the buyer. Or not, that is your choice. The thing is, a true professional can help you in any way you need, only charging fairly for the services provided. A commission-only salesperson on the other hand, can only get a commission if they convince you not to sell privately and to instead list your property with them.

What is your agent's Job Description?

Assuming you do want the help of an agent? Remember, being clear about what you want is the first step to achieving anything. First comes the goal, then a plan (a proven formula, a recipe) to achieve the goal, followed by competent actions.

It's no different when it comes to engaging an agent. Before you hire one, you'll first need a job description to be clear about exactly what it is you expect them to do for you. Your job description dictates your hiring process. First define the role, then invite people (who believe they have the skills to fulfil that role) to apply. Narrow down the applicants to a short list, interview them to ensure they can do what is wanted, and lastly it's wise to check their references before finally hiring the best match for the position.

This is all common sense, yet when it comes to selling a home, common sense often goes out the window. Many make the mistake of selecting an agent based on the wrong criteria, because they didn't clearly define what they expected from the agent in the first place.

If your goal is simply to sell, then you will probably ask prospective agents…*Can you sell our house?*.

This is where you could start being led down the wrong path. The focus will shift to all the reasons they can sell your property better than the next agent… *we have the biggest team, we do the most advertising, we sell the most, we have the most buyers, we have a guaranteed sale program, we have this fancy new gimmick, list with us and go into the draw to win…*

The point is, it's not a matter of *who* can sell your property, as anybody can sell it. You don't even need an agent – you can *just sell it* yourself.

Some sellers focus on selecting their agent based on their quoted price. *How much can you sell our property for?*

This is also dangerous. While getting the best price is the second step to maximising profit, focusing on this alone may lead to selecting the agent that quotes the highest price – the agent that *tells you what you want to hear*.

There is a big difference between telling you a high price, and actually achieving it. The first is nothing but words plucked from thin air. The second requires a proven formula, a plan, and of course the skills to implement that plan competently.

If your goal, however, is to bank the most profit from the sale, then your selection process will revolve around exactly that. Your interview will be focused on ensuring the agent has a proven formula, combined with the skills needed to to maximise your net profit.

Instead of asking *Can you sell my property?* or *How much can you get …* wiser questions would be: *How will you maximise our profit? Outline your proven formula to maximise our selling price and reduce our expenses? Please show me recent case studies of your approach in action and supply me with references from previous clients.*

Before you hire an agent, there's another very important thing to be clear about. Do you want them working for *you* or *a commission?* Do you want them to advise you what you *need to know* or tell you what you *want to hear?* Do you want a straight-talking *consultant* or a hungry *commission-only salesperson?*
The answer to those questions will dictate who you select and how you engage them.

This is a Crossroad

If you are like most home owners, and hate listing presentations, those empty sales pitches that include a salesperson coming to your house, sitting at your kitchen table, talking you into the traditional one-size-fits-all solution, followed by attempts to close for your signature, then I believe you will find a Professional Service Approach refreshingly different. It's not pushy. It's more transparent. It gives you choices, but more importantly, it's proven to get our clients better results.

An advisor certified in the The Common Sense Approach is different from what you'd expect of salespeople. They have rejected the sales culture and committed to being a true *professional*. They are not there to talk you into anything – so you won't get any slick scripts, sales lines or manipulative closing techniques. Instead, they are genuine about using their inside knowledge and experience to your advantage.

However, before we can help you, first we must understand your individual circumstances. So our client process starts with getting to know you with a detailed and comprehensive diagnosis of your situation and needs. Instead of turning up under the guise of a Free Market Appraisal, gushing about your property and leading you into the *tell you what you want to hear* trap, we use a more sophisticated approach, that makes more sense. But, if you're set on a free appraisal, and not much concerned about getting professional guidance and maximising your profit, our advice to you is simple: you should speak to a different agent, seek out another agent to work with. Not us with our common sense approach.

A professional approach is different. We ask questions.

Like your doctor, we can't possibly give you a prescription until there is an accurate diagnosis. Without a diagnosis, it's malpractice. It's unethical. This is why a comprehensive diagnosis is so critical - not just to maximise your health with your doctor, but to maximise your net profit from the sale of your home.

When it comes to you, your family, and your financial future, we refuse to cut corners. Some clients say, *It's no big deal, cut a few corners*, but that's not how we operate. Also, some homeowners are not accepted as clients because we differ in our belief about how to best sell their home. If it's not a good fit, then why force a round peg into a square hole? So much of success is about teamwork. Maximising your profit requires that we are on the same page and want the same result.

Sometimes, clients don't like what we have to say, but at least it's the truth. Good news, bad news, it doesn't matter, we will only tell you the truth. I could be wrong but I believe that most people appreciate the truth, and when they hear it, say to themselves: *It's about time. Thank you.*

Maybe you've had that reaction while reading this book. I hope so. The truth isn't always pleasant, but armed with the truth is the only way anyone can ever consistently make smart decisions. And it's the only way to prevent clients from making *fundamental* mistakes that expose them to unnecessary risk.

Most homeowners hope for a pleasant and profitable home sale experience, but too often, many are not willing to do the required legwork to ensure that that hope becomes a reality. Hope is not a strategy anyone can depend on.

The bottom line is: the choices you make about your home sale, how you choose to prepare your home, how you choose to price your home, which overall strategy you choose and who you choose to represent you, are yours. I suggest that, if maximum profit is a priority, then do as much research as you possibly can. It's this willingness to do so that sets our clients and their results, apart.

If you're the type of person who appreciates the truth and want a professional on your team, the process starts with a Real Estate Consultation. There is no cost for this initial consultation, nor is there any obligation to become a client. Not on our part or yours. It's simply an opportunity to discover your needs and determine if our approach is a good fit for you. If not, no harm done; at least you will be armed with the truth. And the promise from us – there will be no gimmicks, sales pitch, no pressure and definitely no corny closes – just genuine advice.

Regardless of what anyone says, the true secret in achieving a successful home sale, as well as success in life and in your finances, is being informed.

CHAPTER EIGHT

THE THREE PILLARS FOR MAXIMISING PROFIT

At the beginning of this book I proposed rejecting the hype, lines and gimmicks pitched by the traditional industry. Banking the most from your sale doesn't involve hype and it's not about gimmicks. It's about three things:

1. Avoiding costly mistakes,
2. Increasing your sale price, and
3. Reducing your expenses.

That's it. That's the secret.

But before we focus on those three pillars… have you ever noticed all the bookshelves when you visit your solicitor, filled with volume after volume of case law, or all the medical books at your doctor's office?

When seeking specialist advice, although I expect them to know what's contained in all those books, I certainly don't want them to tell me every single lesson. Plus those they've learnt through real-life experience dealing with thousands of clients or patients. It would take years to convey all that knowledge. And the large majority of it would be irrelevant to me. Instead, I want them to advise me of only the parts that are relevant to my situation – so I can make *informed* decisions.

Similarly, this section is not about outlining all the possible scenarios, potential mistakes, choices of strategies, selling methods, and the like. That would take volumes. This is simply an overview, giving some insight into the areas that do effect your net profit, and how an agent acting as a true professional can help you tailor a solution that best fits with you.

The First Pillar For Maximising Profit:
Avoid Costly Mistakes and Traps

The biggest losses home sellers suffer, are due to costly mistakes and traps. Sometimes they reduce your selling price, sometimes they increase your selling costs. Sometimes both. But either way, they strip your equity, leaving you less in your pocket. Just like the sellers in *'If only they knew'*, they're often 'hidden losses'. Meaning you don't even realise you've dropped tens of thousands of dollars.

Obviously your best protection from costly mistakes is to avoid them in the first place. To do that, you first need to be aware of them.

But sadly, many of them are laid by the industry, in it's persuit of commission. You are bombarded with propaganda, misinformation and half truths. Since you might only sell one or two homes in your lifetime, it's hard for you to know what to believe, and how it really works behind the scenes. Which is why, if pushed to pick one thing that causes sellers the most harm, it would be...

Being naive about how the industry works.

So I believe, whether navigating sensitive legal matters, choosing the best medical treatment or selling your home... protecting you - helping you avoid costly mistakes - is a key function of any professinal service provider. You are relying on them to use their specialist knowledge and experience to your benefit. To safely guide you through the maze.

It's a partnership that depends entirely on trust. To be effective you need to know they have your interests at heart. I mean think about it, if you don't trust their motives, how can you trust their advice? And if you don't trust their advice, why on earth have you engaged them in the first place?

The Second Pillar For Maximising Profit:
Increase Your Selling Price

Many factors affect your final price. Some, like the economic climate, the number of buyers in the market, and amount of competition, are outside your control and therefore not worth losing sleep over. However, those you can control fall into eight categories. We've already covered the first four… Being clear about what you want; Putting the right overall strategy in place; Which agent you engage, if at all; and Avoiding costly mistakes and traps. Following are the other four:

5. Pre-market Preparation

This involves two parts, which many sellers underestimate the importance of - at their peril.

<u>Presentation</u>: Bottom line, the presentation of your property will affect your final selling price. The more work and attention you pay to key areas, the better. It really will pay dividends.

There are simple ways to add value to your property before it goes to market. There are also improvements that will cost you more than they will return and are therefore not worth the effort or expense. The trick is to know the difference.

A quick google search will reveal plenty of resources on what to focus on. So I'm not going to regurgitate it all in this book. I think you'd rather me stick to the knowledge you can't find elsewhere.

However, I do want you to understand how MASSIVELY important it is. Especially in this day and age, where buyers often inspect the photos online before deciding if they will inspect your home in person. You may have seen plenty of photos advertisied that instantly put you as a buyer off. Don't make that mistake with your home sale.

The photos of your property are now more important than ever, and the best way to ensure great photos, is to first put the effort into getting your presentation spot on. Even the best photographer in the world can't make a tip look immaculate. For that you'd need a photoshop wizard. But even they can only do so much.

<u>**Remove Road Blocks:**</u> This is about removing any issues that may hold up your sale, give the buyer ammunition to negotiate a lower price, or even scuttle your sale altogether. You want to make it as easy as possible for the buyer to buy. The more obstacles you can remove, the better.

CASE STUDY: Dale and Tina

Dale and Tina did everything right when selling their property. They achieved a quick unconditional sale, for more than they expected and saved $8,910 in fees – thus substantially increasing their net profit. How did they do it? What strategies did they implement to such great effect? We can't share all of the steps in this one case study, however there is one simple tip every seller can implement before going to market - that can have a huge effect on the whole selling process and ultimately increase your profit:

Order your own L.I.M Report (Land Information Memorandum) before you put your property on the market, and make it available to the buyers from day one.

The fact is that today, very few buyers will purchase a property without first checking and approving the LIM report from the local district council. In the standard sale and purchase agreement, the LIM clause allows for 15 working days for the buyer to order and approve the LIM. So from the point of accepting an offer on your property, you have to wait three weeks before knowing if the sale is unconditional. This creates several potentially damaging issues:

1. In my experience, the more conditions in a contract, and the longer the time frame for those conditions, the higher the chances the contract will fall over. People often get what's called buyer's remorse. The longer they have to dwell on it, the more likely they are to have second thoughts and look for ways to pull out. By making the LIM available we can often shorten the LIM clause from three weeks to one week, or even remove it entirely.

2. If, after three weeks waiting for the LIM report to be approved, a problem is then discovered, several things can happen:

- It may scuttle the sale all together. In which case you are left holding the baby and have to find another buyer for your property. In the eyes of other buyers, it appears you have been sitting on the market not selling for a further three weeks, which damages the perception of your property (*Why hasn't it sold yet?*). This can put downward pressure on your price and lead to a lower offer second time around.

- The buyers often use the issue in the LIM to renegotiate a lower price. You are put in the no-win position of having to choose between losing the buyer or reducing your price in order to secure the sale. This needlessly erodes your value.

- You may have to go through the process of rectifying the issue in order to get your offer unconditional. This can hold up a sale for a further 3-5 weeks while you arrange repairs or remedies and deal with council red-tape and procedures. Not only will this add stress, but while you are doing this, your time on the market is lengthening which increases your selling costs (legal fees, marketing costs etc) and further adds to the perception that your property is not selling.

By having the LIM up front we can often eliminate these potential issues. For a start, if there is a problem with the LIM then, as the seller, you are much better off knowing about it first. You are then in control of your choices. You can go about rectifying the problem before you go to market, thus removing the issue completely, or still go to market, but transparently disclose the issue to the buyers up front. Thus making it clear that your property is offered for sale *as is* and has been priced accordingly.

In this way, the buyers make their offer knowing about the issue in advance, there are no nasty surprises for them to discover that could scuttle the sale. It also effectively removes their ability to use the known issue as leverage against you − to try and renegotiate a lower price at a later date.

Two more things ...

Buyers love the transparency of sellers providing the LIM report up front. One of buyers' biggest fears is the old saying... *Buyer beware*. In their eyes, by providing the LIM, it shows that you, as the seller, are not trying to hide anything. Further, a major law of marketing is *make it easy to buy*. The fewer hurdles buyers have to jump in order to purchase, the better. This one small thing puts the buyers more at ease, making them more likely to offer you a better price with fewer conditions up front.

Finally, if you choose our Professional Service based fee structure, where the quicker your property sells, the less you pay, by providing the LIM, we can often reduce the time on market. This helps you save even more fees and therefore increases your profit. All round it is a win/win for you.

So why wouldn't you order your own LIM report before you go to market? Interestingly some agents advise you not to. Their school of thought seems to be: *If there is a problem with the LIM and we know about it – then as agents we have to disclose it to buyers.* In other words they are saying: they would rather not know about the problem and hope that the buyer doesn't discover it. This has proven to be terrible advice.

It perpetuates the distrust of agents and sellers by the buyers, making them more wary, slower to make decisions and more likely to add further conditions to their offer. Secondly, most buyers will check the LIM anyway, and if they do not intend to, then under the Real Estate Agents Act, we are obligated to advise them to do so. Therefore, the chances of the problem (if there is one) not being discovered by the buyer are very slim. In our view, advising clients to use a strategy that will fail in 95% of cases, does not make sense.

Maybe agents tell you not to provide the LIM up front, because they don't want to wait two or three weeks before placing your property on the market. They want their sign-up as soon as possible. Again we disagree with this thinking. It shouldn't be about rushing to the market so the agent can get a commission quicker. The focus should be on what's best for you, our client. The pre-market preparation is too important to rush. It will have a huge effect on the outcome of your sale, so we'd rather you hold off going to market until you have everything perfect. Then you are more likely to get a better, quicker result and maximise your net profit.

If paying for the LIM is a financial struggle for you, we can cover the cost in the meantime. If you are just trying to save $300 by getting the buyer to pay for the LIM, then that is your choice, however we recommend you re-read this case study.

It's also wise to apply this approach to any other potential roadblocks. For example, here in New Zealand pre-1935 homes will need an electrical inspection in order for the buyer to secure insurance. Why not also get that sorted in advance?

Part of our job is to help you identify any of these issues that may hold up a sale. The more we can remove before going on the market, the better your chance of maximising your profit and minimising your stress.

6. On the market

Once you have your overall strategy in place and preparation complete, you are ready to launch to market. While on the market, several factors will affect your end result.

Method of sale:

There seems to be a lot of different selling methods to choose from: Private Treaty, which is basically having a Set Price; Tender; Deadline Sale; By Negotiation; Auction... However they essentially fall into two categories. Price or No Price. But which is the best for you?

Of course, like anything, none of them are perfect. They all have their upsides and downsides. They all work best in different situations. The thing to be careful of is that Salespeople are good at giving all the so called positives of their favourite method, but they seldom reveal the negatives. This is classic sales behaviour - offerring just the information that stacks your decision in their favour, rather than empowering you to make balanced decisions by giving you the whole picture.

In the medical world this is called 'Informed Consent'. If a Doctor, for example, recommended a treatment without disclosing the possible side effects, it would be considered malpractice. In a nutshell, this is the fundamental difference between a true professional and a salesperson.

No price marketing seems to be in vogue at the moment. You may hear lines such as: *'Don't set a price limit on your property - somebody might offer you way over the odds.'* And yes they might. I've seen it happen - occasionally. But most often they don't. The salesperson has neglected to reveal that many buyers ignore properties without a clear asking price. Meaning if you don't transparently display a price, you could loose up to half of your enquiry.

Further, with no price to go off, buyers are forced to look at your 'Rateable Value' for some sort of guide. Which in our neck of the woods tend to be low. Meaning you're often attracting buyers who either cannot afford what you want in the first place, or are pitching their offers based on a low starting point. That's not good.

In summary, there's no perfect method of sale. Just make sure you are getting the whole picture before choosing.

Smart Marketing - Attracting Buyers:

This is about attracting the best buyers in the most cost effective way - while keeping your property special, protecting it's perceived value and not damaging it with 'over exposure'. Here is what's really important when it comes to marketing:

Professional photography: Don't skimp on this - just do it.

Target marketing: A classic marketing mistake is trying to make your advert appeal to everybody - a shotgun approach. Smart marketing is about laser focus. Both in who you are trying to attract and where you market. Poorly written copy placed in a medium where none of your potential buyers are looking - is a total waste of money.

Cost vs Return: This is closely related to 'Target Marketing'. Some advertising may look great but cost a lot while getting very little return. Agents glossy in house magazines are a classic example. Do not pay for them. They are nothing but a profile building exercise for the agent, at your expense. Oh and don't get me started on the line 'Just one premium buyer will more than pay for the cost of your advert' - I hope you can see through that one.

Emotional connection: People buy emotionally. Listing a bunch of features inspires nobody. The secret is to wrap benefits into a story - creating an emotional connection with the buyers.

The Three P's: Presentation, Price, Promotion. Without getting the first two right you are pouring money down the drain. No amount of advertising will sell a poorly presented and overpriced property.

Test and Adjust: It astounds me how often I see the same property advert running for months, sometimes years. If your ad has been running for several weeks with little to no enquiry, there is a problem. Please fix the issue and re-test. As they say, doing the same thing and expecting a different result, is the definition of insanity.

How inspections are handled:

By Appointment Only vs Open Homes? This is personal preference and just like with 'methods of sale' they both have pro's and con's. 'Open homes' for example may get more bodies through your home. They just won't all be real buyers. With 'by appointment only', you will have less people peeking in your wardrobes, but they are more likely to be pre-qualified and genuine.

The main thing to understand is that you do not have to have Open Homes. They are mainly recommended by salespeople because they are a good prospecting tool - a way for them to meet other potential sellers, who are just checking out the market before selling their own.

How buyers questions are answered:

Why are they selling? How long has it been on the market? Are they negotiable?… may seem like innocent questions from a buyer. But beware, how they are answered can influence their offer. For example, if as a buyer the salesperson disclosed that the seller was 'On transfer in two weeks and very keen to get something on paper'... Has your opening offer just increased or decreased?

Have a back-up plan:

What if your initial strategy and approach is not working? What if you are getting low interest or offers? What then? It's important to think about this before you launch to market. Then if it happens, you are ready to adjust. The worst thing is to wallow and do nothing - hoping it will work out. Hope is not a strategy.

The reason for being on the market in the first place, is to get to the point where one or more buyers want to buy your property. This leads into one of the most important parts.

7. The Negotiations

As you discovered in Chapter Five , the way traditional real estate salespeople negotiate often undersells their clients' property. This is because they use an Offer - Counter Offer style of negotiating. Take a look at the diagram below… It shows the process and how it plays right into the buyer's hands.

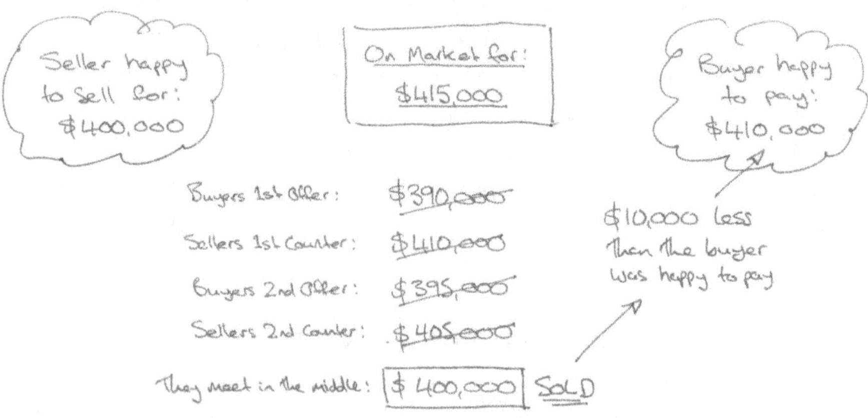

Clearly a buyer wants your property as cheaply as possible. Their goal is to find your lowest price. So they start low and work their way up until you say yes.

The problem is, this style of negotiating focuses on the least you as the seller will take, instead of the most the buyer will pay. It usually drags you down further than the buyer up. Bottom line, it often leaves money in the buyer's pocket, money that should have been in your pocket. (Just like in the true story *If only they knew*).

From the salesperson's point of view this style of negotiating certainly gets a deal. It secures a commission as quickly as possible.

Over the years we've developed a unique style of real estate negotiating. One that is far superior to the traditional style because it focuses on finding the buyer's absolute highest price. It can therefore add thousands of dollars to your net profit. But of course, I would say that. Unfortunately it can't be 100% proven. Two or three separate agents cannot negotiate the same transaction with the same buyer at the same time, making it impossible to prove which really is the best style. About the closest you can get to a Key Performance Indicator of an agents negotiation ability is their **Negotiation Success Rate:** On average, what percentage of their clients' asking price do they achieve during negotiations? I would happily put ours up against any other traditional agent in the world.

Should you decide to engage an agent certified in the Common Sense Approach, they will clearly demonstrate this superior style, showing how it works and how they will implement it on your behalf.

8. Troubleshooting

Once you've accepted an offer – it's still not time for celebrating. As they say, *it's not over until the fat lady sings*. It is not SOLD until all conditions in the contract have been met, that is, until the contract is what's called 'Unconditional'.

The timeframe between accepting an offer and that offer becoming unconditional, is when things can fall apart. Inspection reports can put a spanner in the works. The buyer's finance may be declined. The Land Information Memorandum (LIM) may show up a problem. There are often situations where contracts need to be renegotiated, or troubleshooting needs to be done, in order to save the sale. This is where your Pre-Market Preparation and having an advocate in your court can pay huge dividends.

The Third Pillar For Maximising Profit:
Reduce Your Selling Costs

If you've avoided costly mistakes and done everything possible to maximise your sale price, the only other way to increase your net profit is to reduce your expenses.

COMMON SENSE TRUTH #24
Any expense that doesn't add value is eroding your profit

As you've now discovered, an inefficient industry, unnecessary advertising, poor negotiations and fundamental mistakes all increase your costs and therefore erode your profit. The problem is, with the traditional way, you have no way of controlling those expenses because they are bundled together into the selling fees.

Commission-Only

Although commission-only offers you the option of not having to pay for services unless your property sells, it creates some major issues:

- Creates a 'conflict of interest' - who are they really acting for?
- Commissions are mainly why it costs so much when you do sell.
- Genuine sellers subsidise the work done for non-sellers.
- Higher-value sellers pay more for the same job than lower-value sellers...

On this point, the ease of sale, regardless of value, usually comes down to how well you present your property, how realistic your price expectation is, and how many genuine buyers are in the market. The value of your property has nothing to do with the amount of work involved in facilitating the sale. Yet with traditional real estate commissions, if you're a $400,000 seller, you pay twice as much as your friend across town selling a $200,000 property. It doesn't make sense, unless you believe the notion that just because your property is worth more you should pay more for the same service.

- **Commission removes your ability to reduce your expenses.**

Remember the *Tale of four home sellers*, because of Ken's smart decisions and actions, his property sold easily with less work required than for Clare, and yet he paid the same fee. Now if you are like Ken, are serious about maximising your net profit, you'll be interested in another way of doing things:

Professional Service-based fees

Rather than paying your agent a commission based on the value of your property, how about paying them fees as you would any other respected professional service provider? Fees that more fairly reflect the expertise, time and outgoing costs involved in servicing just your needs. User pays. In other words, the easier your property sells – the less you pay. It's simply a more efficient and fairer model.

- **You only pay for the work and marketing done on your behalf instead of subsidising the work being done for others.**
- **You're not supporting the time and effort salespeople spend looking for sellers (prospecting).**
- **You're not paying a premium for having no risk.**
- **You have more control over the entire selling process, with a range of strategies and services to choose from.**
- **It removes the conflict of interest created by the traditional commission-only model. Thus your best interests and your agent's are aligned – you are both working towards the same goal.**
- **It enables you to reduce your selling costs and therefore increase your profit.**

We have developed such an approach. You are given the choice of a more efficient fee structure. A combination of consulting fees, outgoing costs, hours worked and a bonus (a little like a profit share – based on how much extra you bank compared to the less efficient commission-only way).

In fact this is the structure the 161 sellers employed to net an extra $756,328 more than they would have under the traditional commission-only model.

Let's quickly go back and apply it the clients in *A tale of four home sellers*:

Ken: would have benefited for his smart decisions and actions by keeping $6,000 more than under the traditional commission-only model.

Clare: even though she needed more work than Ken, she still would have netted $3,600 more than under the traditional model.

Bob: would have netted around $1,000 more than under the traditional model.

Larry: would've paid the most fees. Although in reality we wouldn't have accepted him as a client.

Perhaps if the entire industry worked on a Professional Service basis Larry would have thought long and hard about wasting everybody else's time and resources, in which case, the industry wouldn't need to recoup from the genuine sellers the losses they incurred for Larry.

Of course, like everything in life it's your decision. Traditional commission or Professional Service based fees? The main thing is that you understand the difference and have a choice that gives you more control over how much you net from your sale.

CHAPTER NINE

A FEW QUESTIONS ANSWERED

So how much are our fees exactly?

Our fees can be anywhere from a few hundred dollars to thousands of dollars. It depends on exactly what you need from us and how much work is involved in helping you.

How much extra net profit will you bank?

Every client is different, so we can't promise, or tell you exactly how much better off you will be, until we know more about your personal situation and your property. What we can tell you, is that on average the extra net profit banked per client is currently just over $4,700. Or put another way, it's proving to be on average 36% more efficent for our clients than a traditional commission.

How do we calculate the extra net profit?

It's very simple. We measure it against what you would have banked after all expenses, had you chosen to engage us under the traditional *commission-only* model. For example, Mark (Part Five) sold for $356,000. On a traditional commission he would have paid $12,652 leaving him $343,348 net in his hand. Under our Professional Service-based structure his fee was $7,493 (including paying us a bonus), leaving him $348,507 in his hand. This is $5,159 extra in his pocket.

What if it doesn't sell?

Why wouldn't it sell? The only reason would be if you chose not to. It's up to you – remember, you hold the power. If you are not genuine about wanting to sell then you may be wise not to go to the market. And the last thing you should do is wallow on the market long-term.

What if we go to market then choose not to sell?

Will we still need to pay some fees? If you choose our pure Professional Service-based fee structure, then the short answer is yes. Just as if you went to your solicitor for legal advice, then later chose not to follow that advice, you still compensate him for his service. This is no different from any other service provider.

This may be a foreign way of thinking for the real estate industry, but it's how every other respected profession works, and it is a proven model.

It makes you consider more seriously what you want in the first place. Putting your property to the market on a whim, is never wise.

It also encourages you to be careful in selecting who you engage to serve you. You are likely to do more homework beforehand, making sure you are 100% comfortable, knowing we are the best you can possible have working on your behalf. When it comes to real estate, listing with just any salesperson can be very costly.

Ironically, engaging us on a Professional Service basis - that ultimately helps you net more - takes a considerably higher level of trust from you in our integrity, and belief in our ability. While the low trust commission-only model creates a conflict of interest and strips so much more of your equity than is needed.

If you don't trust or value your agent's expertise enough to at least fairly reimburse them for the advice, work and expenses incurred on your behalf, why would you allow them to take a large percentage of your property's value? It doesn't make sense.

That being said, you have choices. You can choose traditional commission-only warts-and-all – which will leave you with the least in your pocket; a pure Professional Service-based fee structure – which will leave you with the most; or a combination. The point is, a true professional can structure the fees in a number of different ways depending on your personal situation and circumstances. What's most important is that whatever fee structure you choose is transparent, clearly understood, and agreed upon up front.

What if it takes a long time to sell?

Good question. 'Time on market' and 'work done on your behalf' are not necessarily related.

If you present your property at its best, and price it realistically, you will get more inspections in the short term than if you choose to wait at a level above the current market.

Take Bob and Beryl for instance (see Part Four). For them we implemented a strategy designed to maximise their profit in the short term. The seven hours of direct work we did on their behalf, from the first buyer across their doorstep to unconditionally sold, was concentrated into a period of less than two weeks. Anne-Marie and Bernard on the other hand were in no hurry (see Part Five). For them we implemented a strategy designed to maximise their profit while waiting for the right buyer. The slightly more than eight hours of direct work done on their behalf was spread over six months.

Now, if you are employing the second strategy, as long as you are not hounding your property with expensive and needless advertising, your selling costs will not blow out of proportion.

If you are worried about this, we are more than happy to cap your fees at the traditional level – so there is no way it will cost you more than a traditional commission. We can offer this because we have never had a seller where our Professional Service-based fees have worked out higher than a traditional commission.

What if there are no Approved Restate Advisors or agents following a Professional Service Approach in our area?

If you are genuine about selling, have taken steps to present your property at it's best, and have realistic price expectations - then every real estate agent in your area wants their sign on your fence. Remember you hold the ultimate power. You are the paying client - therefore you can control the terms of how you engage your agent. You do not have to give in to the way they've always done it.

The first step is to find an agent you feel comfortable working with. Don't initially worry if they are a traditional commission-only agent - that doesn't mean thay are bad people - they often just don't know any dfferent. Then why not ask them to read this book before discussing with them how you'd like to engage them.

Both you and your preferred agent are welcome to contact me for some ideas on smarter ways to structure the fees to create a win/win for you both.

If you can't find any agents you want to work with or that are at least open to discussing fairer fee structures with you - then consider selling privately. In this case (within New Zealand) we can still help you remotely. Giving you background guidance and advice throughout the process.

PART FOUR

The Common Sense Approach in Action

Some Case Studies

Frank and Val buying and selling

"We were thinking about moving but did not want to be rushed. So we invited Carl to come and have a chat. After listening to our concerns & discussing different options, he suggested & laid out a plan that was best for us & our situation. It made a lot of sense & put us in control, so we could go along at our own pace. Carl & Liz worked closely with our solicitor to make sure we were protected. They helped us throughout the whole process including advice around buying our next property privately. They were never pushy & we always felt they had our best interest at heart. We ended up with several offers within a week of putting ours on the market & sold for more than we had planned. Their new fee structure also saved us $4,900 compared to traditional fees. This meant we ended up with a bit extra & could comfortably buy our new home without having to touch our savings. We couldn't be happier with the team at Restate."

Frank and Val are simply all-round good sorts. They've worked hard, paid their dues and are enjoying their well-deserved retirement.

When we first met Frank and Val, they had decided it was time to downsize but loved the home they were in and didn't want to move unless they found the right unit. The problem was, the sort of units they wanted were in short supply and didn't last on the market. They knew when they did find *the one*, they would more than likely miss out to another buyer before they had a chance to sell their own.

There was also the issue of finances. They couldn't know exactly how much they could afford to pay for the next home until they had an offer on their own. The last thing they needed was to overextend and have to dip into their retirement fund.

Some agents had suggested selling first, but the thought of being forced to leave their much-loved home without knowing where they were going was understandably distressing. What if they couldn't find the one? Would they be forced to panic-buy? They could probably stay with family, but didn't want to impose on them – *they're busy enough making their own lives.* The motor camp? Or rent until the right one comes along? No thanks, one move will be big enough, let alone two. Further, in a rising market, the longer they remained renting the more their buying power would be eroded. So what to do? It was a classic *rock and a hard place* situation.

Once we identified what was most important to Frank and Val, we put a plan in place that gave them best chance of moving with the least emotional and financial risk. The overriding strategy was simple.

First, get their property ready for sale *before* they started seriously looking for another one. This involved slowly working on some needed maintenance and getting their presentation as perfect as possible. Once that was complete we had the photography done, marketing plan in place and their property fully-loaded into our system ready to launch to market in an instant. A LIM report was also ordered on their property to help speed up the sale process when the time came.

Step two was an in-depth analysis of their finances, including an unbiased appraisal. The key here was financial safety. They needed to make sure once they started looking they were working on a realistic to conservative budget. There was no point in looking at other properties they were unlikely to be able to afford, or that meant they had to achieve more than the market would pay for theirs.

They were now ready to find their next home – with no time pressure. It didn't matter if it took a week or six months, the moment they found a property they wanted (within their budget), they were in a strong position to jump. We could have their property on the market within a matter of hours – giving them a head-start on other buyers who were not as well prepared. They knew that when the time came they would need to have an offer on theirs within two weeks or they'd probably miss out.

The back-up plan was also simple. Should they miss out on the property, then theirs would come off the market until such time as they found another. We would repeat this process until they were safely in a new home, but there was no way they would be out on the street. The keys were preparation, safety and no pressure. This strategy worked so well for Frank and Val that it has become a template we've now successfully deployed for other clients in a similar situation.

Bob and Beryl: $53,000 more than they wanted

How does something like this happen, you ask? Let me first take you back, so you have some insight into Bob and Beryl's situation.

Going into the first discussion with a client, we never know what to expect. Sure, we can pull information about the property, its sale history, size, rateable value and recent comparable sales, but it's almost impossible to predict what we are going to find. The most important part of the puzzle is the clients, whose specific needs, goals and reasons for wanting to sell are unique.

And that's why it baffles me that most agents go into their initial meeting with not only a predetermined idea of the price, but a one-size-fits-all approach both to selling it and to their fees. No assessment, no diagnosis or questions, and no choices, just a canned presentation and a lot of assumptions.

We take a different approach – in our eyes, the only responsible one to take. We come to the first meeting armed with a blank pad, our own curiosity and a list of questions to ask. Experience tells us that before we can even begin to discuss an accurate prescription, we must run a battery of tests. I've said it before: *prescription without diagnosis is malpractice.*

Within seconds of walking in the door, I could tell this wasn't a spur of the moment decision. Bob and Beryl had a plan. The house was absolutely immaculate – A++. They were in the middle of touching up minor paint imperfections and old sheets were down protecting the new carpet in high- traffic areas.

Cup of tea in hand, sitting around the dining table, we got to the most critical part. What were Bob and Beryl wanting to do? What was most important to them?

I won't share their private business, but they wanted to sell *yesterday*. Their major concern was *could they actually sell it?* They'd seen similar properties wallowing on the market for months and didn't want to suffer the same fate. Also interesting was their price expectations. It's seldom we come across clients who have a low opinion of their home's value.

After an hour of discussions, questions, some recommendations, and ensuring we were all on the same page *(after all it was not only important that I understood their needs, they also needed to be comfortable with us and how we work)*, I left to prepare an in-depth market analysis and tailor a recommendation.

By our second meeting Bob and Beryl had already actioned earlier recommendations. Final presentation was almost complete, the LIM had been ordered and the photographer was booked. An electrician had been arranged to inspect the wiring and provide a written quote for any work required to bring it up to insurance company standards. Most insurance companies now require that wiring in pre-1940 homes "must have been replaced within the last 30 years". If the buyer can't get insurance, their finance won't be approved and the sale could fall over.

It is better to know what you are dealing with before you go to market, rather than discovering a major issue after accepting an offer, which spins you into 'damage control'.

It turned out that there was $6,000-$8,000 worth of wiring work required. Bob and Beryl were worried. Would this hold up the sale? Would they need to do the work before they went to market? How long would it take to get the work done?

Because they wanted to sell sooner rather than later, we decided a transparent approach was the best solution. We would go to market disclosing the wiring work required and providing the quote up front. That way, buyers could make their offers knowing full well they would also need to immediately invest a further $6k - $8k.

Taking that into account, we recommended an ideal market strategy including an initial asking price. To my utter surprise they vetoed me. *"No Carl, we want to sell and are happy to accept lower than that. We do not, under any circumstances want to still be here in two months' time".* I immediately went on record that the price they planned to ask, in my opinion, was under-market, and again suggested they start higher. However, as long as they've been given transparent information, have fully considered their options, and what they instruct is ethical, we are ultimately here to follow through on their decisions.

Clearly this wasn't a matter of would they sell or not? Bob and

Beryl had already decided that. It was more about how quickly they sold, what price they ended up getting and how much their fees would be?

It would have been so easy to write up the first offer on day one, then clip the ticket for a large percentage of their equity. But that's not what we are about. Our duty is to maximise how much they bank. Even though they wanted a quick sale, I wouldn't sleep at night if we allowed them to leave funds on the table.

There was no doubt this needed to be handled correctly to protect them. I agreed to go ahead on the condition that before considering any offers, they would allow us enough time to give all genuine buyers the opportunity. Further, for their situation our Professional Service-based fee structure would be more efficient than a traditional commission. They agreed, we shook on it, and a launch date was set.

As you can imagine, upon hitting the market, it caused quite a stir – people accused us of *purposely underpricing* and *trying to drive local real estate prices down.*

As expected, within days, several buyers were pushing us to present just their offer (excluding others) close to asking price. Within the week a total of 23 buyers viewed the property. Six registered their interest, four of whom drafted contracts in a *best offer* situation.

The winning bid was totally unconditional, with a possession date to suit our clients and a whopping $53,000 over what Bob and Beryl would have happily accepted. We were confident it would sell for more, but nobody could have predicted that much more.

We invested $550 dollars in marketing, and from the first buyer crossing the doorstep to it being unconditionally sold, we did just under seven hours of direct work on Bob's and Beryl's behalf.

This case study is instructive. It offers numerous lessons to achieving a great result when selling your home:

Prescription without diagnosis is malpractice

Your personal situation, needs and wishes are unique. They deserve a tailored approach to both strategy and fee structure. Beware agents pushing one- size-fits-all. They are not *consulting with you*, they're *selling you.*

Take the time

Make the effort to present your property at its best. Or pay the price.

Preparation is the key to avoiding disaster

Identify and prepare for any potential issues that may hold up a sale, *before* going to market.

Transparency does wonders for your bottom line

Open and early disclosure of any issues you have not already fixed is vital. Provide recent reports and written quotes for any major repairs needed. Hide nothing. If you don't try to pull the wool, neither will the buyers.

Value is an opinion

It's subjective and charged with emotion. What something is worth to you is different from what it's worth to the next person. Therefore no one, can possibly tell you what someone else's opinion might be in advance. Ultimately, only two opinions count – yours, as the seller, and the buyers'. Your agent's job is to bring you the buyer with the most favourable opinion.

Strategy and Competent Execution jointly rule the roost

Regardless of where you as a seller choose to price, with the right strategy in place, and the sale competently handled by someone acting in your best interests, it's almost impossible to undersell your property.

Choose your counsel carefully

Bob's and Beryl's sale could very easily have been butchered by a hungry salesperson chasing a quick and easy commission.

Paying a large percentage of your equity to an agent

Regardless of the work involved, is unnecessary. Even including a healthy bonus for helping them net more, Bob's and Beryl's fees were close to half what they would have paid in traditional commission. They are better off and we were still well-rewarded for serving them. That's a win/win.

PART FIVE
Some words from our Heroes

As of writing, The Common Sense Approach has helped 161 clients collectively bank over $750,000 more than they would have under the traditional way. This approach is quickly becoming the choice for sellers who appreciate genuine advice. Through word of mouth, the number of clients joining the revolution is steadily growing. We feel blessed that the approach has been independently judged a winner by our local Business Excellence Awards.

However, if you are considering working with an agent certified in The Common Sense Approach, but don't personally know us or don't have a friend or family member who has worked with us before, then I encourage you to do your own research. Don't just take my word for it. Ultimately, it's what those who have experienced the approach have to say that matters most.

If you are interested you can find many more of our client case studies at: **www.restate.nz/clients**

Aaron & Belinda banked $5,704 more.

When we decided it was time to sell our house we spoke to a few different real estate agents. After speaking with Carl and hearing about the Restate way of selling, our decision was easy. We like that the team are working to try and change the real estate industry and give people better value for money and with the bonus of being local...

Jess & Dan banked $4,804 more.

When Carl explained his new real estate model to us it was a no brainer , it made perfect sense... The result speaks for itself with our home selling for $11000 over asking price and saving $4800 on our fees.

Mark banked $5,159 more.

We chose Restate to sell our property for two reasons:1. The price advantage over traditional commission methods, and just as importantly 2. The confidence we got from the agent when discussing Restates philosophy and methods. The price advantage was realised & we enjoy the fact that we have only paid for the service required to sell our house. Nothing more, nothing less.

Neville & Kay banked $12,258 more.

It wasn't just the huge savings in commission we knew we would be making, it was also their outstanding professionalism and their sage advice. Everything resonated with us which made us decide to go with Restate. They are committed to working for you as the seller

Justin banked $5,318 more.

Why did we decide to go with Restate? The key was how black and white Restate's model and philosophy is. It connects with you, it's positive and it works! How confidential the team were was outstanding. This is a team who care about the seller ... On top of all that, our fees were close to half what we would have paid a traditional agent.

Bernard & Ann-Marie banked $10,891 more.

The Restate team was really good to work with. They were obviously always working in our best interests and we knew where we stood at all times.

Kay & Graeme banked $10,822 more.

We considered our options of selling our home & were impressed by Restate. Our home didn't take long to sell & Adam kept us clearly informed along the way. We felt very comfortable working with Adam who made selling our home a simple, stress free experience. We would recommend the Restate System to anyone considering selling there property.

Bob & Ali banked $6,590 more.

When we decided to sell our family home of 15 years, we thought long & hard about who we would engage to market it for us. Restate's fee structure was the deal breaker for us. It was just commonsense to pay for a professional service rather than a flat commission rate. This was followed up with professional & honest service, with frequent & open communication.

Annie & Brian banked $5,159 more.

We had a fantastic time selling our property with Restate. Adam took the time to get to know us and what we wanted to achieve. We felt he and his team were open, straight forward and most importantly, honest. We will recommend Restate and most definitely, we will look forward to working with them in the future. Many thanks.

Kim banked $5,123 more.

I felt very comfortable and excited about how his model of real estate selling could work for me and all the while leaving me with more money for our next purchase. The team were all very professional to work with and kept me informed through the process. I would definitely recommend them to anyone who is considering selling.

Dale & Tina banked $8,910 more.

Restate's new system of selling real estate has proven to be a fantastic new concept and a complete success for us. The consultancy method we chose made for simple easy to understand fee structures and a clear outline of what to expect. When you're ready to sell your home there's no doubt you should give Restate a call first, if you're serious about keeping more of your hard earned money in your pocket.

David & Rae banked $6,410 more.

We were keen to engage Restate to market our home. It turned out to be a great decision and with Adam Dufty's expertise the sale was actioned almost immediately. We found Adam to be very caring, informative agent who also steered us carefully through the mire of purchasing another property else where. And the savings we made were an added bonus.

PART SIX
Role of Honour

The 161 pioneering clients who have helped positively change the world of real estate by proving the Common Sense Approach consistently creates superior results.

They are the real heroes of this story.

01.	Elizabeth & Bill	Saved	$885
02.	Craig & Gaela	Saved	$7,502
03.	Ross	Saved	$3,176
04.	Lisa	Saved	$3,020
05.	Stacey	Saved	$5,219
06.	Logan	Saved	$262
07.	Paul	Saved	$2,960
08.	Nick & Jenny	Saved	$3,643
09.	Ashlee	Saved	$377
10.	Charlotte	Saved	$3,894
11.	Rae & David	Saved	$6,410
12.	Emily & Blair	Saved	$4,937
13.	Robert & Charles	Saved	$1,431
14.	Bryan & Noeline	Saved	$3,165
15.	Shayne & Christine	Saved	$2,134
16.	Sarah	Saved	$4,662
17.	Sue & Laurence	Saved	$7,027
18.	Patsy & Janet	Saved	$4,595
19.	Stephen	Saved	$3,049
20.	Kim	Saved	$5,123
21.	Kay & Neville	Saved	$12,258
22.	Lorraine	Saved	$527
23.	Bill & Gail	Saved	$8,721
24.	Sani & Diane	Saved	$4,539
25.	Jock & Lorraine	Saved	$4,232
26.	Sam	Saved	$3,658
27.	Nigel & Peggy	Saved	$9,241
28.	Jakki	Saved	$609
29.	Donna	Saved	$5,678
30.	Andrew & Andrea	Saved	$6,001
31.	Rene & Richard	Saved	$2,746
32.	James	Saved	$4,419
33.	Leanna & Cole	Saved	$3,676
34.	Colin & Raewyn	Saved	$6,482

35.	Julian & Fiona	Saved	$6,667
36.	Deborah & Aaron	Saved	$4,777
37.	Emit & Marcel	Saved	$6,390
38.	Donna	Saved	$552
39.	Tracey & Barry	Saved	$4,711
40.	Kingan Family	Saved	$2,192
41.	Michael & Gloria	Saved	$2,847
42.	Gail	Saved	$2,949
43.	Linda & Brian	Saved	$6,346
44.	Vaughan & Kirstie	Saved	$5,430
45.	Brendon & Michelle	Saved	$6,557
46.	Les & Tracey	Saved	$7,796
47.	Chris & Dave	Saved	$4,728
48.	Bob & Beryl	Saved	$6,901
49.	Dawn and Paul	Saved	$4,416
50.	Anna and Bernard	Saved	$10,891
51.	Craig	Saved	$6,507
52.	Jason	Saved	$4,381
53.	Dean	Saved	$1,759
54.	Bob and Margaret	Saved	$3,495
55.	Heather and Bob	Saved	$5,520
56.	Deborah and Noel	Saved	$1,869
57.	Lois and George	Saved	$4,992
58.	Bill and Joyce	Saved	$6,471
59.	Kevin and Fiona	Saved	$1,307
60.	Rosalie	Saved	$4,639
61.	Anthony	Saved	$1,733
62.	Jonathon	Saved	$3,100
63.	Aaron and Belinda	Saved	$5,704
64.	Christine	Saved	$4,641
65.	Neil	Saved	$5,793
66.	Judith	Saved	$5,246
67.	Julie and Evan	Saved	$5,502
68.	Rae Family	Saved	$3,751

69.	Jo-Ann	Saved	$6,466
70.	Grant and Steph	Saved	$6,919
71.	David and Robyn	Saved	$7,363
72.	Deidre	Saved	$1,522
73.	Donna	Saved	$6,545
74.	Craig	Saved	$5,628
75.	Peter and Gloria	Saved	$6109
76.	Daniel and Jessica	Saved	$4,804
77.	Ray and Kathleen	Saved	$3,116
78.	Christine and Terry	Saved	$13,249
79.	Lee and Kiri	Saved	$3,009
80.	Chris and Dave	Saved	$642
81.	Ross and Delwyn	Saved	$6,555
82.	Olivia	Saved	$3,907
83.	Hayden and Bex	Saved	$1,328
84.	Linda and Graham	Saved	$5,123
85.	Michael	Saved	$4,194
86.	John and Barbara	Saved	$267
87.	Graeme and Judith	Saved	$10,882
88.	The Withell Family	Saved	$7,157
89.	Kathy and Jeff	Saved	$9,512
90.	Rachel and Hamish	Saved	$2,851
91.	Susan	Saved	$4,254
92.	Pete and Suzie	Saved	$3,741
93.	Marilyn	Saved	$948
94.	Tony and Sonia	Saved	$331
95.	Sheryl	Saved	$5,771
96.	John and Jan	Saved	$8,793
97.	Margaret	Saved	$5,190
98.	Sue and Geoff	Saved	$4,431
99.	Grant and Maureen	Saved	$7,640
100.	Justin and Kelly	Saved	$5,358
101.	Katherine	Saved	$5,869
102.	Ken	Saved	$7,554

103.	Ann	Saved	$5,702
104.	The Butler Family	Saved	$3,056
105.	Karen and Nathan	Saved	$4,326
106.	Tony and Debbie	Saved	$4,922
107.	Doris	Saved	$3,225
108.	Vicki and Stephen	Saved	$520
109.	Karlee and Craig	Saved	$4,019
110.	Elizabeth	Saved	$5,639
111.	Mark	Saved	$5,159
112.	Andrew	Saved	$2,047
113.	Anita and Brian	Saved	$2,341
114.	Michelle	Saved	$818
115.	Shulay and Grant	Saved	$3,504
116.	Joan and John	Saved	$6,637
117.	Bob and Alison	Saved	$6,590
118.	Trevor and Penny	Saved	$9,260
119.	Keith and Janice	Saved	$6,825
120.	Michael	Saved	$8,283
121.	Moana	Saved	$1,440
122.	Kevin and Leanne	Saved	$2,731
123.	Sharon and Steve	Saved	$1,630
124.	Doug	Saved	$5,112
125.	Teri	Saved	$2,900
126.	Nick	Saved	$1,708
127.	Gale and Ewen	Saved	$2,792
128.	Mrs Bennewith	Saved	$1,169
129.	Ross	Saved	$1,937
130.	Dale and Tina	Saved	$8,910
131.	Deb and Nick	Saved	$3,935
132.	Val and Frank	Saved	$4,968
133.	Warren	Saved	$5,759
134.	Orcilla and Cornelius	Saved	$3,955
135.	Ross and Delwyn	Saved	$9,878
136.	Roger and Arohanui	Saved	$2,282

137.	Catherine and Ross	Saved	$11,655
138.	The Milne Family	Saved	$3,441
139.	Anne and Jeremy	Saved	$7,230
140.	Barry	Saved	$875
141.	Simon and Angela	Saved	$4,393
142.	Anthony	Saved	$1,840
143.	Derek	Saved	$6,942
144.	Aaron	Saved	$2,339
145.	Chris and Dave	Saved	$4,094
146.	Barry	Saved	$3,924
147.	Max and Heather	Saved	$4,513
148.	Pam and Murray	Saved	$4,912
149.	Robert and Judith	Saved	$6,486
150.	Jo and Jonathan	Saved	$4,217
151.	Nancy	Saved	$4,355
152.	Stephen and Sarah	Saved	$7,487
153.	Nigel	Saved	$8,800
154.	Alison and Sash	Saved	$1,905
155.	Shaun and Jane	Saved	$1,000
156.	Colin and Raewyn	Saved	$11,280
157.	Thelma	Saved	$2,960
158.	David	Saved	$2,287
159.	Elizabeth and Marty	Saved	$7,875
160.	Glen and Ann	Saved	$6,274
161.	James and Clare	Saved	$6,201

$756,328

PART SEVEN

A message for agents

Fellow agents, if you have read all the way through this book without burning it, then I applaud you. I understand that many of the truths contained herein are hard pills to swallow. The reality is: our industry, in the eyes of consumers, is simply not trusted. You are seen as a self-serving salesperson before you even walk in the door.

Now you might say it's *only a minority of agents that give the rest of us a bad name*, but the issue runs much deeper than that and, like it or not, we are all tarred with the same brush. Even if you do genuinely care about doing what's best for your clients, there are two big problems with the traditional way.

Firstly, they don't believe you. Can you blame them? After all, you are a commission-only salesperson. How can you reasonably expect them to trust your advice? Secondly, the way our industry traditionally works makes it hard for you to truly act in their interests in the first place. If you've been in this industry more than five minutes, you know this is true. Often, what's best for your client, means you don't get a commission. You don't feed your family. Your survival is on the line. This creates a basic conflict of interest between what's best for you and what's best for them.

Then there is the sales culture. We all know our industry publicly preaches *acting in our clients' best interests*, but look at the reality, how it really works behind the scenes. Look at what you are required to do to survive. Look at what you are taught – the sales training, the scripts, the closes, how to increase your profile, and the prospecting. You are expected to cold-call, door-knock and act like an annoying tele-marketer, all of which further erodes your reputation.

The reality is, the large majority of your time and effort is spent looking for and persuading sellers to list with you. Once you have the listing, as long as it's well-presented and priced right, the buyers come. It sells itself. Sure, a good agent can make a difference, but deep down you know that if that seller had listed with a different agent, they will still sell.

So the industry is not really about protecting and serving your clients. It's about winning the listing, then persuading them to accept the market, so that you, your agency and franchise can get a commission.

Are you taught how to truly 'add value' – what really helps increase your client's sale price, or reduces their selling expenses and therefore maximises their net profit? No, it's all focused on getting that commission and building your profile.

Now look at what the industry celebrates. Is your success and quality as an agent judged on how much extra net profit you put in your clients' pockets, their satisfaction with your services, how much value you added to their lives, or the positive word of mouth you are creating?

Again, no. Awards are given for gaining the most listings, the most vendor-paid advertising and so on. Success is judged on your gross commissions – because that's what the establishment cares about. That is what is important to the franchises, the bigwigs at the top. And they keep recruiting more and more around you. The name of the game (for them) is being the biggest and having the most salespeople, which continues to erode your position. This makes it increasingly competitive with more and more chasing the same fees, making it harder and harder for you to graft an honest living. But it works for them; they keep on clipping the ticket regardless.

We are finding there are two distinct types of individual agents out there:

1. Those who want to break free

They are in this industry because they genuinely want to make a difference in their clients' lives. They gain a sense of pride from helping clients achieve their goals in the most efficient way possible, seeing them as people to be cared about and protected, not a lead to be converted nor a commission to be closed. They want to be part of a true profession. They want to build a legacy they can be proud of. They are not prepared to sell their soul and do much of what the sales culture expects of them. Invariably they are therefore not the so-called top producers.

Seeing what really goes on behind the scenes drives them crazy. They hate being tarred with the same brush as those who put their commission above what's best for their client. They'd love to break free of their association with the traditional industry, but are stuck in the system. The traditional way gives them no alternative. Sadly many of these agents end up leaving to find a career that does resonate with their true character.

2. Those who love the 'Sales Culture'

They are the quintessential smooth-talking salesperson. They thrive on it. They are unashamedly in this industry chasing the commissions. They love the thrill of the chase, the big egos, the profile, the chest-beating, the prospecting, the slick lines, the pressure, and the dog-eat-dog environment. For them it's a numbers game. *Always be closing* is their mantra. This industry sings their praises, puts them on stage, turns them into coaches and encourages the rest of you to be more like them.

The question is, which are you?

If you want to break free

It seems we are on a similar page. At Restate we are on a mission to elevate the real estate industry into a true profession, one that puts the interests of its clients above all else and adds genuine value to those it serves. We want an industry our clients can trust and that we, as agents, are proud to be a part of. One that resonates with our character and is about something more meaningful than cold-calling and scrapping over commissions.

However, this requires a shift in thinking. The commission-driven sales culture our industry was built on, is responsible for what it has become. It's why consumers don't trust them and why commissions are so disconnected from the value they give.

We have addressed both issues with one clean sweep by turning our backs on the traditional sales culture and restating what it means to be a real estate agent. All sales scripts and closing techniques have been banned. We stopped traditional prospecting over 2 years ago and are now generating referral business at a rate I've never seen in this industry before.

We've cracked the code. Not only are our clients happier and banking more profit, but we are also better off both financially and reputation-wise.

You undoubtedly have questions about how we have made this work – we are willing to share the answers. A good place for you to start, is by joining the conversation at **www.realestaterestated.com.**

I believe this is a game-changer. It's the future of our industry and I would like nothing more than to see this philosophy spread. In fact I believe it's imperitive for it to spread, if we (as an industry) wish to not only survive but thrive in the comming years of industry disruption.

So if you want to break free of the way the industry currently works, are genuine about putting your clients' best interests above all else, and are excited about being part of a start- up community that's revolutionising the industry, then you may be a good fit with our professional service culture.

As long as you meet our standards, you can apply to become an Approved Restate Advisor. You will obviously need to commit to our values and become certified in the Common Sense Approach (so we can ensure consistently superior results for consumers anywhere).

We are in no way interested in *bums on seats*. We will only accept those with the highest standards of ethics and client care, and who are also passionate about elevating the professionalism of our industry.

Should you be accepted, you will be more like the key partner in your own legal or accounting firm – growing your own practice with our backup and support. It will NOT be a franchise arrangement where head office takes a large percentage of the cream off the top. They are a big part of the problem we are fighting to fix. So we have come up with a much better solution that cuts out many of the traditional inefficiencies, enabling both you and your clients to be better off.

If You love the 'Sales Culture'

That's your choice. For the record, we think differently. In our opinion the traditional commission-only sales culture of your industry is responsible for robbing your integrity. It's the reason why only 10%–20% of consumers trust you, and it's also why your industry is so bloated and inefficient. This is surely a wake-up call that things need to change?

Our new model is now proven to be better for both our clients and us. It's simply more efficient, with our clients banking more than they would have under the traditional model, while our earnings per client are similar to what they used to be. Our appointment to list ratio is substantially higher and our list to sell ratio is close to 100%. But the really exciting thing is that our client satisfaction and referral rate have gone through the roof. Positive word of mouth is spreading fast in the community, so clients are seeking us out rather than the other way around. Our production per agent is close to three times higher than the typical industry – without us doing any traditional prospecting. And the feeling and sense of pride that we are making a real difference in our clients' lives is truly fantastic.

If you love the sales culture then we are probably not your cup of tea. We are leading the industry in a different direction, but wish you all the best of luck.

ACKNOWLEDGEMENTS

Breaking new ground is never easy, but it's ingrained in our kiwi spirit. We are a melting pot of pioneering warriors. We punch well above our weight. We stand up for what's important, no matter how big or loud the opposition.

I think we are doing something special here. And I say "we", because you're a part of it. You – our clients, readers, supporters – are the real heroes in this story. Without you, there's no way we could have ever made this magnitude of difference, in such a short period of time. Without your amazing encouragement, and above all, your help spreading the word, I wouldn't be writing this today. So a heartfelt and sincere 'Thank you'.

To our team: it takes real courage and character to stand up for your convictions and fight against the status quo. Your work ethic, integrity and faith in our mission has been inspirational. Thank you for your dedication. To quote one of my mother's heroes, Margaret Mead: *"Never doubt that a small group of thoughtful, committed people can change the world. Indeed it's the only thing that ever has"*.

Influencers: I wish to thank a few leaders who have helped shape my experience and view on this industry:

Phillip Kennard, who gave me a start as a green 21-year-old. You are still the best boss I've ever had the privilege of working with.

Neil Jenman, consumer advocate, author of *Real Estate Mistakes* and several other great books. You were the first I came across to stand up to this industry, the first voice of reason against the establishment.

You encouraged me to question the *way it's done* and your grounding in ethics has been invaluable. Although we are now heading in slightly different directions, I still and always will respect and thank you for your influence.

Mollie Wasserman, visionary author of *The end of 6%*. We've never met, but your book helped confirm and solidify my direction. I just want to let you know we are continuing to "fight the good fight".

Ryan Fletcher – friend, mentor and inspirational thought leader who has helped me find my voice, and encouraged me to speak out. Thanks my man.

To my family and friends: this section would not be complete without thanking you. Yes I know I'm a dreamer. Thank you for believing. I couldn't have written this without your support and encouragement. Especially my gorgeous girlfriend Kirsty, thank you for putting up with me constantly hiding in my cave :-) xx

CARL SLADE - AUTHOR AND CREATOR

I had that feeling *I don't belong here. This is not my tribe. It's not who I want to be and it's certainly not how I want my business to be.*

I couldn't get out of that typical real estate industry conference quick enough. That was the tipping point - when I finally decided to stop trying to fit in with the establishment and instead stand up for my own convictions.

The very next week I started the process of building a totally new model for the real estate industry. One that is ultimately better for you, our clients, and therefore also us. Looking back, my entire career has been leading to this. Right from the outset I never really fitted the sales culture. I saw how it puts its own interests above those of the client and I wanted to positively change it.

I remember how my grandfather and father did business on a handshake – times when your word was your bond. I believe those types of values need to be put back in front of this industry's thirst for commission.

Over the years I voiced those beliefs. You could say this made me a bit of a rebel, even an outcast. I must admit, there have been times when I was totally disillusioned with how the industry works – feeling like I was losing the battle to make any difference. But rather than leave, I suppose stubbornly, I chose to stay and try to find a way to make the industry fit with my own character. It's been a 25-year journey of trial and error, success and failure, rebuilding, then rebuilding again.

In hindsight, I can't believe it took me so long to put the puzzle together. Those elusive last few pieces, the ones that make it all work, were hiding in plain sight – they just required me to look through a different lens.

Feel free to reach out to me at: carl@restate.nz